DIFFERENTIATED INSTRUCTION

Different Strategies for Different Learners

second edition

LORI ELLIOTT, CHAR FORSTEN, JIM GRANT, *and* BETTY HOLLAS

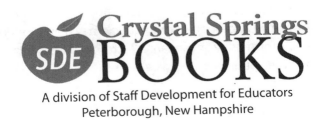

Crystal Springs
SDE BOOKS

A division of Staff Development for Educators
Peterborough, New Hampshire

Published by Crystal Springs Books
A division of Staff Development for Educators (SDE)
10 Sharon Road, PO Box 500
Peterborough, NH 03458
1–800-321-0401
SDE.com/crystalsprings

©2012 Crystal Springs Books
Illustrations © 2012 Crystal Springs Books

Published 2012
Printed in the United States of America
16 15 14 13 12   1 2 3 4 5

ISBN: 978-1-935502-26-5
e-book ISBN: 978-1-935502-28-9

Library of Congress Cataloging-in-Publication Data

Forsten, Char, 1948-
Differentiated instruction : different strategies for different learners / Lori Elliott ... [et al.]. -- 2nd ed.
p. cm.
Prev. ed. entered under Forsten, Char.
Includes bibliographical references and index.
ISBN 978-1-935502-26-5
1. Individualized instruction. 2. Lesson planning. 3. Teaching--Aids and devices. I. Elliott, Lori, 1968- II. Forsten, Char, 1948- Differentiated instruction.

LB1031.F65 2012
371.39'4--dc23

2011047820

Editor: Cathy Kingery
Art Director and Designer: S. Dunholter
Cover Design: Janet Zak
Production Coordinator: Deborah Fredericks
Illustrator: Phyllis Pittet

Over the last twenty years I have been honored and blessed to teach groups of incredible students in the Nixa Public School district. Those first years of teaching fourth grade were especially powerful for me as I grew to understand the importance of providing a positive classroom environment, real-world learning experiences, and individualized instruction. I appreciate all the hard work, laughter, and memories we shared together, and I dedicate this book to my amazing students at the Nixa Public Schools.

—Lori Elliott

I dedicate this book with sincere thanks to Bitty for the lessons she taught me about learning. Perhaps the most important lesson continues to be that we must get to know each child in order to teach each child.

—Char Forsten

In 1969 twin brothers Jim and Jerry entered my sixth-grade classroom. They were "on loan" foster students from a New Hampshire state reform school, and they soon taught me that if they were going to learn, I would need to alter my teaching methods dramatically and differentiate the curriculum in order to meet their learning needs. I am eternally grateful to Jim and Jerry—and to every student who forced me to review my role as teacher—for what they taught me. I dedicate this book to them.

—Jim Grant

"What can I do to encourage more learning in my classroom?" I dedicate this book to four students—Luann, Larry, Brian, and Nathaniel—who continually made me ask myself this question and who probably taught me more in my early years of teaching than I taught them. "What can I do to encourage more learning in my classroom?" It is our hope that this book of strategies will help educators answer this vital question.

—Betty Hollas

Acknowledgments

Special thanks to the following educators for contributing strategies:

Dick Dunning

Gretchen Goodman

Bob Johnson

Contents

Introduction..vii

How to Use This Book........................ix

Management

No Problem!..1

Front and Center......................................2

Student at Work: Do Not Disturb............3

Manage with Music..................................4

Mark with the Sunshine...........................5

"Lefties" Have Different Needs.................6

Plotting Homework...................................7

Choice Charts..8

Listen to Yourself.....................................9

The Eyes Have It!................................... 10

It's a Plan... 11

"One Piece of the Puzzle" Grouping Method ... 12

Help Wanted.. 13

Manage with Popsicle Sticks................. 14

No Can'ts Allowed................................. 15

Student to Student................................ 16

Stand, Move, Deliver............................. 17

Pick Your Presentation Style.................. 18

Community Building

Funny, Sunny Times............................... 19

Class Walkway....................................... 20

Watch Your Tongue............................... 21

Go Wild... 22

Appreciation Circle................................ 23

Praise Behind Your Back........................ 24

Resident Experts.................................... 25

Clock Partners....................................... 26

Mix It, Mix It.. 27

Toothpaste.. 28

We're Going on a Scavenger Hunt!........ 29

Blindfold... 30

Flying High with Praise.......................... 31

The Classroom Buzz.............................. 32

The One and Only Me............................ 33

Well, I Never!.. 34

Teaching Tools

Power Up Your Center Time.................. 35

Talk to Yourself..................................... 36

Twist and Learn with Wikki Stix............. 37

You Can Count on Bingo Chips............. 38

Let the Games Begin............................. 39

Funneling Information............................ 40

Vocal Immersion................................... 41

There's an App for That......................... 42

Highlighting What's Important............... 43

"Post It" with Notes............................... 44

Can You Spot the Learning?.................. 45

Using a Focus Frame to Get the Picture............. 46

Sliding Mask.. 47

Point the Finger..................................... 48

Catch That Word................................... 49

In Praise of Page Protectors.................. 50

Get a Grip on It..................................... 51

Watch and Learn................................... 52

It's About Time...................................... 53

Memorize with Mnemonics................... 54

Quiet, Please! Student at Work.............. 55

Literacy

Enlarge Print and Eliminate
Distracting Artwork............................... 56

Lights, Camera, Writing......................... 57

Familiarity Breeds Attempt 58

Bring It into Focus 59

Human Scrabble 60

Ready, Set, Create! 61

Finding Your Voice 62

First Things First: Cross the Midline 63

Teach in Chunks 64

Digital R.A.F.T. 65

C.A.P.S. Off to Editing 66

Word Clouds 67

4-6-8 68

The World at Their Fingertips 69

Word Map 70

Three Facts and a Fib 71

Splash and Sort 72

In the News 73

C.P.S.R. (Copy-Pair-Share-Respond) 74

Apply a Different Symbol System 75

Colorful Questions 76

Over the Head 77

Partner Pair 78

Pass It On 79

Sticky-Note Symbols 80

Team Windowpane Discussion 81

Digital Scavenger Hunts 82

Money Summary 83

Magic 20 84

Three-Card Write 85

Math

Calculations in a Zip 86

One Strip at a Time 87

Go to the Mat for Learning 88

Teach with Edibles 89

Skill Levels Students Can Deal With 90

Get the Picture 91

Number Relationships 92

Capture Math Facts with Captive Dice 93

I've Got Time 94

Triangular Number Bonds 95

What's My Name? 96

Box One, Circle the Other 97

Keep Your Numbers in Line 98

Cross Out Every Other Math Example 99

Calling All Numbers 100

Numbers in the News 101

Focusing on the Facts 102

Equivalent Fractions Before Your Eyes 103

Howdy, Partner Factor! 104

Not Your Average Math Practice 105

Assessment

What's Your Response? 106

Anecdotal Records 107

Poll the Audience 108

Level the Playing Field 109

One, Two, Three . . . Go! 110

Personal-Learning Time Lines 111

High-Tech Assessment 112

Student-Led Conferences 113

Here's Looking at You, Kid 114

Facts in a Flash 115

Realistic Rubrics 116

Survey Says 117

Dueling Charts 118

Post What You Know 119

Appendix 121

Resources 146

Index 155

Introduction

I f students aren't learning from the way we teach, then we need to teach them in the way they learn.

When the original edition of this book was published, we began with the above statement. We explained that it embodied the essence of what differentiated instruction is all about. That basic premise clearly rang true for many educators, and the book has been very popular.

But many things have changed since this book was first published. Classrooms are more diverse than ever, and you need an ever-expanding toolbox of ideas for reaching all your learners. At the same time, technology now offers a host of options for easing your work with differentiation while making the options more appealing to both you and your students. Clearly, it's time for an update.

In this revised edition, we've brought our favorite strategies up to date, added new ones (including some devoted specifically to differentiating through technology), and inserted additional alternatives where appropriate—all to give you even more options.

What does it mean for an educator to differentiate instruction? It means just what we wrote in the first edition: that the educator knows a variety of effective teaching methods, strategies, and materials that work and has the wisdom to know when and with whom to use them. That goal hasn't changed, despite the ever-growing number of possibilities for reaching it. So, as we did with that earlier edition, let's start with a quick look at differentiation.

A dynamic concept, differentiated instruction challenges the "one size fits all" way of thinking. There is no magic program or one best way of teaching, because there is no one standard student profile. All students are different, and we need different strategies for different learners. That's what this book is all about: different pathways to learning.

Some excellent books and materials are available on differentiated instruction. Carol Ann Tomlinson, widely regarded as the nation's expert, shares the definition, structure, and major ideas in her books and articles. Here is a brief overview of the global strategies associated with differentiated instruction that Carol recommends:

- **Curriculum compacting.** This strategy focuses on student need rather than on textbook structure. It involves assessing students prior to a unit of study to determine what they already know and how well they know it. The teacher then uses the assessment results to make decisions about what the students need to learn.

For example, a fourth-grade teacher might give a math pretest on multiplication with multi-digit multipliers and find that some students already perform this operation fluently, while others struggle with basic facts. The teacher would base his instruction on what the students need, instead of simply covering all pages in the chapter. In other words, some students would require extra study, while others would work through the chapter as is, and still others would work on only a few concepts and then proceed to a higher-level enrichment study.

- **Tiered activities.** These can include lessons, assignments, or both. When there is a wide range of learners in a class and the teacher wants all the students to be grounded in the same fundamental ideas, she can use a tiered activity approach. For this strategy, the teacher first identifies the key concepts and skills all students must know at the end of the unit. Then she chooses different reading materials or selections and matches them to the students' reading levels. All students read about the same topic; they simply use different materials in the process.

  Teachers can also differentiate assignments. For example, all students write a report on the same topic, but one group writes straightforward expository pieces while another group writes higher-level position papers.

- **Learning centers.** These answer the question "What are the other students doing while I'm meeting with an individual or a small group?" Centers are areas in the classroom that can serve as "study labs" or designated places that house materials and anchor activities that supplement or enhance the goals of the curriculum. The teacher need not be present for all learning, and exploratory, practice, and extension activities can be readily accessible for students at learning centers. For example, while the teacher meets with a small group for direct instruction on multiplying with one-digit multipliers, some students practice their basic multiplication facts, while still others work on activities that involve higher-level multiplication skills.

- **Flexible grouping.** This strategy involves creating temporary groups for a particular reason based on students' instructional needs and/or interests. The groups can be created on the basis of either skill levels or interests.

  For example, when working on a community unit, a teacher might divide the class into groups according to their interests in the different community roles. Instead of having all students study all community roles, each small group focuses on an in-depth study of one role. A culmination includes having each group present its findings to the rest of the class. Everyone learns, and everyone teaches!

- **Mentoring.** The highest level of understanding is obtained from teaching others. When children support, or scaffold, each other, they affirm and verbalize what they know, put the information into a context as they explain it to others, and strengthen their self-esteem by proving their competence.

The goal of this new edition is to give you even more options for specific, practical strategies, materials, and ideas that support the major components of differentiated instruction listed above—and to show you how you can put them to work in your classroom tomorrow. We hope that in the pages that follow, you'll find just the strategies you need to continue your journey into differentiation.

How to Use This Book

We want you to be able to access what you need without having to read from cover to cover, so this book's design, like the writing, is intended to save you time. You'll find separate sections focusing on management, community building, teaching tools, literacy, math, and assessment. Just turn to the section that addresses your immediate need, look for the grade ranges applicable to you, and grab the idea that looks most appealing. Here are some key features to watch for:

Section of book—identify at a glance the category you want

Grade range—quickly find what's most appropriate for you

Reproducible—find the ready-to-use reproducible that supports the strategy

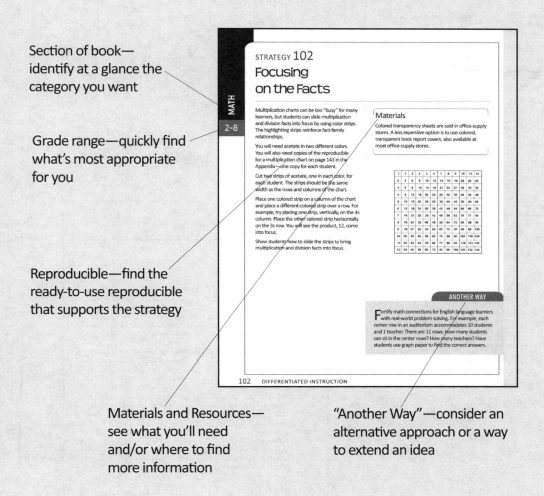

Materials and Resources—see what you'll need and/or where to find more information

"Another Way"—consider an alternative approach or a way to extend an idea

Not every strategy calls for every one of these key elements, but we've tried to include each one wherever we felt it would be most helpful.

Do you prefer to scan from back to front? If you find yourself intrigued by a particular reproducible and wondering about the strategy it supports, just look in the side margin of the reproducible to find the connection. Or turn to page 121 for a complete list of what goes with what.

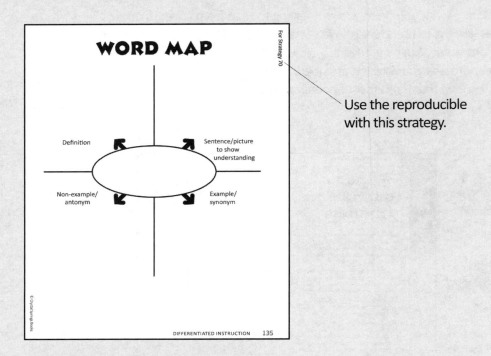

Use the reproducible with this strategy.

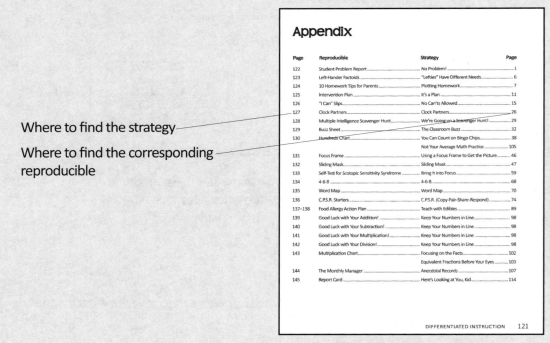

Where to find the strategy

Where to find the corresponding reproducible

Still looking for more? Check out the extensive list of resources at the back of the book for more great reading on the topics considered here.

You want to offer every student multiple pathways to success. We want to do the same for you, the educator. The strategies that follow are intended to do just that.

STRATEGY 1

No Problem!

This management idea helps minimize tattling and also assists students in thinking through problems on their own.

Tell students that unless they see "blood or bones," they are to report any problems using the Student Problem Report found in the Appendix on page 122. Many students will look at the report and decide the problem is not that important. Some will begin to fill it out and then realize that it is not that important. A few students will fill out the form and will then think through the conflict resolution on their own.

Younger students can tell the problem to a stuffed animal you have identified as a good listener.

Student Problem Report

Filed by: _____

Date: _____

Description of problem: _____
_____
_____

Location of problem: _____

Persons involved: _____

Witnesses: _____
What did the witnesses do? _____

How do you feel about what happened? _____

How do you think the other student feels? _____

List two things you might have done to solve the problem or prevent it from happening:

1. _____

2. _____

What do you think the teacher should do about this problem?
_____

Student signature: _____

STRATEGY 2

Front and Center

Q: What types of learners prefer sitting toward the back of the classroom?

A: Slower learners, shy students, students with behavior problems, discouraged learners, and students with learning disabilities.

It is easy to understand why some students avoid sitting near the front of the class. This self-protection mode helps them avoid being exposed as potential failures.

Help students understand the advantages of sitting up front by pointing out the benefits. A student seated near the front of the class is:

- in close proximity to better-performing students
- more likely to receive a greater share of the teacher's attention

- able to more easily see the board
- able to hear much better
- better able to know "what's going on" in the classroom
- less susceptible to being distracted from schoolwork
- likely to be more productive and happier with school

Back row:
The back row usually becomes the seating area for shy kids who try to avoid being called on; it's also a breeding ground for disruptive students.

Front row:
Students receive the most attention from their teacher when they sit in the front row but may earn the label of "teacher's pet."

Back row:
The back row is also an area where students may be easily distracted and led astray by friends.

Window and door seats:
Students—even the best students—will become distracted by action and noise coming from outside or in the hallway.

STRATEGY 3

Student at Work: Do Not Disturb

This strategy helps those students who are easily distracted by classroom stimuli to concentrate on their work.

Secure a 24-inch-high piece of cardboard across the front and around both sides of a student's desk with duct tape. This "private office" will screen out visual distractions that take students with attention problems off-task. To add prestige to this adaptation, attach a sign that says "Private Office" to the piece of cardboard secured to the front of the desk.

Always secure written permission from the parent or guardian before attaching a carrel to a student's desk.

Materials

Ready-made desk carrels are available from teacher stores and teacher-supply catalogs.

STRATEGY 4

Manage with Music

Use the power of tranquil music to manage your classroom. Welcome your students to your classroom with brain-friendly background music. Establish the level of your music as the standard for the acceptable noise level in your room. Peaceful music has a calming effect that creates an atmosphere of tranquility.

Music can also be an effective way to transition your students from task to task or from place to place. The length of time the music is played sets the transition time frame.

STRATEGY 5

Mark
with the Sunshine

Checking errors with a red marker tends to be a harsh way to focus on a student's mistakes. Instead try marking correct answers in yellow. This is a good way to celebrate and focus on a student's accomplishments.

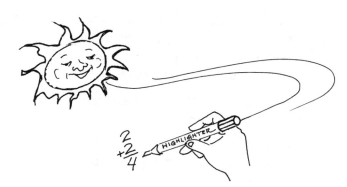

In an alternative approach, highlighted math examples left uncorrected signal the need for rework. Give students as many opportunities as necessary to produce a perfect paper. Indicate on the back of each paper how many tries the student needed to reach proficiency. This reminder is helpful when recording the student's process, progress, and work habits.

STRATEGY 6

"Lefties" Have Different Needs

Being left-handed in a right-handed world can be difficult and challenging for some students. To help them meet the challenge, provide left-handed students with the following:

- A left-handed ruler (no more fingers covering the numbers).

- Pencils/pens for lefties (the lead/ink is non-smudge). There are also pens for lefties with ink that dries instantly.

- Special left-handed scissors.

- Notebooks for lefties (bound on the right; pages are three-hole-punched on the left).

Allow lefties to slant their papers in whichever way is most comfortable for them when writing.

You might like to share with students the list of factoids for lefties in the Appendix on page 123.

Caution: Never attempt to convert the handedness of a student.

Materials

Teaching supplies and materials are available through the following websites:

lefthandzone.com

anythingleft-handed.co.uk

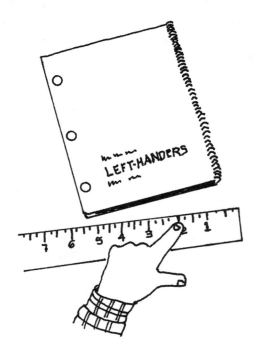

STRATEGY 7

Plotting Homework

Establish homework guidelines that are reasonable for students, parents, and teachers. Homework should be relevant and should support and expand the student's course of study.

The amount of homework deemed reasonable has been debated for decades. National experts on homework suggest that an appropriate amount of homework per night is 10 minutes of work multiplied by the student's grade level.

You might want to share with your students' parents the 10 Homework Tips for Parents reproducible in the Appendix on page 124.

ANOTHER WAY

Some students (and parents) question the value of homework. To foster cooperation, begin by communicating your purpose and goal(s) for each assignment via your class website or school-to-home newsletter. Be sure to include a calendar and provide timely feedback on all homework assignments.

STRATEGY 8

Choice Charts

Anchor activities are meaningful tasks that students can undertake while the teacher is working with other learners or when they have completed an assignment. The Internet offers a wide variety of possibilities for anchor activities. Choose ones that are tied to your content and instruction and that incorporate some form of accountability. To make the activities more appealing, present them in choice charts designed for all learning styles and readiness levels.

Organize the choice chart by types of activities and provide links to the appropriate websites from your blog or class website. Update menus periodically to coordinate with your instruction and your students' changing needs and interests.

Resources

Discovery Puzzlemaker: discoveryeducation.com/free-puzzlemaker
Make-your-own word puzzles

Jigsaw Planet: jigsawplanet.com/
Create-your-own jigsaw puzzles using photos

Crayola Digi-Color: crayola.com/coloring_application
Drawing on the web

Build Your Wild Self: buildyourwildself.com/
Games for creating your own wild characters while learning about animals

New York Philharmonic: nyphilkids.org
Composing music, learning about famous composers, and trying musical instruments

San Francisco Symphony Kids: sfskids.org
Learning about music and instruments

Pic Lits: piclits.com
Using pictures to inspire writing

Toasted Cheese: toasted-cheese.com/webcal/webcal.cgi
Writing prompts

Magnetic Poetry: magneticpoetry.com/
Online equivalent of the magnetic game

Learning Games for Kids: learninggamesforkids.com/word_games.html
Learning games

Vocabulary Spelling City: vocabularyspellingcity.com/
Spelling games and tests

Quizlet: quizlet.com/
Create-your-own flash cards and game playing based on your content

Study Stack: studystack.com/
Create-your-own flash cards

Choice Chart

Puzzles	Music	Fun with Words
Discovery Puzzlemaker	New York Philharmonic	Magnetic Poetry
Jigsaw Planet	San Francisco Symphony Kids	Learning Games for Kids
		Vocabulary Spelling City
Art/Creativity	Writing	Flash Cards
Crayola Digi-Color	Pic Lits	Quizlet
Build Your Wild Self	Toasted Cheese	Study Stack

STRATEGY 9

Listen to Yourself

Resiliency is the capacity to withstand adverse circumstances. Positive and procedural self-talk can be an important contributor to building this capacity.

Discouraged students and students who have "learned helplessness" often give themselves negative messages that are damaging at best.

Teach students to give themselves a "pep talk" before engaging in a task or difficult situation.

These little messages can have a big impact on the student's attitude and well-being. Procedural self-talk helps students remember the steps necessary to do a specific task (e.g., divide, multiply, subtract, check, bring down, and remainder).

Procedural self-talk is helpful for students who have difficulty with task completion.

ANOTHER WAY

To help English language learners benefit from positive self-messages, share your own with them. (For example: I ate a good breakfast, and I feel more alert this morning.) Write your message on the board, and invite students to add their own or record them in personal journals.

STRATEGY 10

The Eyes Have It!

The direction in which a student's eyes are cast can provide important cues for instruction. For example, if a student is visually processing information, you might ask him questions containing words specific to vision (e.g., look, see, visualize).

If a student's eyes indicate auditory processing, questions containing words pertaining to hearing, sounds, and listening would be helpful.

Directionality of the eyes is not an absolute. The illustration shows what is true for right-handed students and how this pattern is reversed for left-handed students.

Because looking upward can activate visualization, students appreciate having informational posters placed on the ceiling and near the top of the classroom walls. (Be sure to check local fire codes before hanging posters.)

Resources

Brain Compatible Strategies by Eric Jensen (San Diego, Calif.: The Brain Store, 2004)

A Framework for Understanding Poverty by Ruby Payne (Highlands, Tex.; aha! Process, Inc., 2005)

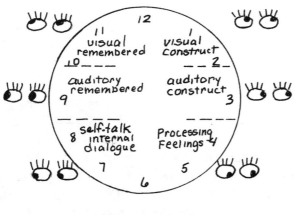

Left-Handed

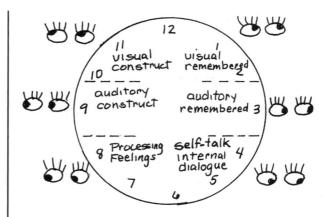

Right-Handed

STRATEGY 11

It's a Plan

Develop a practical "road map" to success for your school's Response to Intervention (R.T.I.) framework. The form on page 125 in the Appendix provides you with a reproducible, non-binding, non-legal format to create an Intervention Plan for students. This individualized plan outlines each student's target area, tier level, and recommended intervention(s). It also includes a chart for monitoring student progress, with space for anecdotal notes. This user-friendly document is straightforward—minimizing paperwork while maximizing the focus on interventions and results.

Intervention Plan

Interventionist/Teacher: _____

Target Area _____

Tier _____ Intervention _____ Initial Status _____ Goal _____

Progress Monitoring Data

DATE	Freq/Duration of Intervention	Results	
			Anecdotal Observations

Interventionist/Teacher: _____

Target Area _____

Tier _____ Intervention _____ Initial Status _____ Goal _____

Progress Monitoring Data

DATE	Freq/Duration of Intervention	Results	
			Anecdotal Observations

Interventionist/Teacher: _____

Target Area _____

Tier _____ Intervention _____ Initial Status _____ Goal _____

Progress Monitoring Data

DATE	Freq/Duration of Intervention	Results	
			Anecdotal Observations

Adapted from Intervention Documentation Folder

© 2008 Gretchen Goodman

STRATEGY **12**

"One Piece of the Puzzle" Grouping Method

This method allows students to work in groups to complete an in-depth study of one aspect of a thematic unit. When student projects are complete, group members present theirs to the entire class.

To begin, decide what part of a study unit is appropriate for puzzle grouping and choose how many topic groups you will create.

Name the groups according to their topics and then draw a master puzzle on poster board, with the number of pieces matching the number of student groups.

Cut out the puzzle on the poster board and give one piece of the puzzle to each group.

You may also purchase large pre-made puzzle pieces.

Each group researches its topic and then reports to the class by a designated deadline. Group members also label and customize their puzzle piece in preparation for the presentation.

As each group gives its report, it attaches its piece of the puzzle. Groups continue giving their reports until the entire class puzzle is assembled.

For example, your class might be working on a community study. Rather than having all students study all the community roles, divide the class into groups to research the jobs of police, firefighters, health workers, government workers, and public-works employees.

Materials

Community Puzzles (pre-made puzzle pieces) are available through compozapuzzle.com.

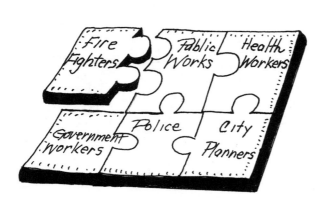

STRATEGY **13**

Help Wanted

This tool helps students signal, without interrupting the teacher or standing in line, that they need assistance.

To make the "Help Wanted" sign, each student takes a sheet of 8 1⁄2" x 11" paper, holds it landscape-style, and then folds it in half.

The student then prints "Help Wanted" in bold letters on the lower half of the paper.

The next time a student needs help, she simply places the sign in front of herself for the teacher or another student to notice and then continues working on the current or alternate assignment.

This is an unobtrusive way to provide individual help in the classroom.

Some students may be unaware that they need help in order to complete an assignment accurately. As they work, invite them to share their progress with you. Use that sharing time to address questions, clarify instructions, and monitor understanding.

STRATEGY 14

Manage with Popsicle Sticks

Place each student's name on a Popsicle stick or tongue depressor. Keep all the sticks together in a stack.

Use the sticks as a handy reminder to say each student's name every day. This can also be a quick way to select students for group activities. Picking a name from the stack is a good technique for randomly calling on students.

When a misbehaving student sees you remove his name from the stack, he knows he must mend his ways. That student's goal is to see that the stick with his name goes back into the stack. This is an effective non-verbal way to correct a student without a confrontation.

STRATEGY 15

No Can'ts Allowed

This idea helps students focus on what they can do instead of what they can't.

Take a tin can and cover it with white contact paper.

Write the words "I CAN" in bold letters on the side of the can. This is the class's "I CAN" can.

Establish a rule in the classroom that no one is allowed to say "I can't." Tell them they just haven't learned it yet.

When a student is able to perform a new skill or a targeted behavior, instruct her to fill out an "I Can" slip. (Teachers can also participate.)

The "I Can" slip should have a space for the student to write his name, the date, and a brief description of the skill or behavior that has been attained. You can make your own slips or use the form in the Appendix of this book (page 126).

Celebrate when the "I CAN" can is filled with success slips!

ANOTHER WAY

Record your students' successes and post them on a class bulletin board. After modeling the process for a week or so, have students compose their own positive "I Can" statements to add to the collection. Encourage them to consider expressing their messages through rhymes or illustrations.

STRATEGY 16

Student to Student

Have each student find a partner; ask the pairs to stand together. You then give an instruction, such as "elbow to elbow." Students are to touch elbows with their partners.

Then give another instruction. For example, you might say "foot to foot." The students no longer touch elbows, but now they touch feet.

After a few directions like the above, you say, "Student to student." Each student then quickly finds another partner—and the partner can be you. The student who is left becomes the one to give the instructions.

This game generates laughter, releases some energy when students need a stretch break, and can be used to form pairs for an instructional activity.

STRATEGY 17

Stand, Move, Deliver

Select any content you want students to process.

Ask students to write for three to five minutes in response to the prompt you give them.

Possible topics might be:

- What has confused you today?

- What have you learned in [fill in subject] today?

- If a new student joined our class tomorrow, what would you tell her about what we are studying in math?

After the students finish writing, play some music. Ask the students to stand when they hear the music and move around the room. When the music stops, ask each student to find a partner and share what she wrote (i.e., "deliver" their writing). Continue this for a few rounds until each student has had a chance to share with several different partners.

ANOTHER WAY

Engage all learners by playing a game of Encore. You'll need a small cloth ball or bean bag. Begin by stating one concept your students learned this week. Then toss the ball to a seated student who states another idea. In turn, that student tosses the ball to another seated student, who repeats the process. Continue until everyone has contributed an idea.

STRATEGY **18**

Pick Your Presentation Style

A typical research project involves students collecting information and then displaying their understanding through media such as posters, essays, or PowerPoint presentations. In many cases, every student is expected to do the same thing.

To differentiate instruction, allow each student to choose a presentation mode that conveys information in a way that suits his learning style and interests. The Internet can help you support student presentations from beginning to end.

Begin by providing clear expectations for the project—use a site like Rubistar (rubistar. 4teachers.org) to create rubrics for students. To help students plan their presentations, select graphic organizers and calendars online at Freeology (freeology.com). As they do their research, have students pay attention to how the information is organized for the reader and how accompanying graphics, illustrations, and animations help them understand the information. Once their research is complete, students can create their own quality pre-entations using web tools or traditional print options.

Online Presentation Tools for Students

Glogster: edu.glogster.com
Digital poster creator

Mixbook: mixbook.com/edu
Digital photo books

Prezi: prezi.com
Zooming presentation tool

Yodio: yodio.com
Podcasting using cell phones

STRATEGY 19

Funny, Sunny Times

Building a positive learning community takes more than a few ice breakers during the first weeks of school. Helping each student feel successful and important is an ongoing challenge, but students will take academic risks when they feel secure with their teacher and classmates. That's why it's essential to nurture what you've begun by building in daily time for laughter and positive interaction.

To maintain community and add laughter to your classroom, take five to ten minutes daily for a class meeting to introduce humorous video clips, games, activities, and songs. Many online resources provide fun activities for the whole class to share together. Through play, students develop healthy bonds of friendship and cooperation, and they learn to respect a variety of individuals and learning styles.

Sources for Online Games and Activities

Ghoulie Games: greenghoulie.com

Origins Online:
originsonline.org/res_classroom.php

Ultimate Camp Resource:
ultimatecampresource.com

STRATEGY 20

Class Walkway

Enhance the self-worth and increase the level of security of students who are experiencing a difficult time in their lives.

Ask your class to make a walkway by forming two equal lines three feet apart. Have the student who needs a "boost" walk slowly through the walkway while classmates express words of encouragement. Give token gifts (e.g., stickers, snacks, pencils, or trinkets). Freely give gentle pats or make other appropriate gestures that show signs of caring.

The student enters the walkway "emotionally unsettled" and emerges "emotionally supported."

STRATEGY 21

Watch Your Tongue

What is said and how it is said can have a major impact on how a student learns. Always use kind words and a gentle manner to direct, guide, and correct students.

Negative messages are counterproductive and affect the way the brain processes and stores information.

Make a conscious effort to avoid any messages that might be perceived by students as threatening.

Classroom threats include:

- Embarrassing students
- Giving unrealistic deadlines
- Insensitivity to students whose English is limited
- Bullying/harassment
- Calling on students who don't know the answer
- Punitive discipline
- Unfair comparisons to other students
- Requiring students to read aloud

STRATEGY 22

Go Wild

Brainstorm a list of animals. Make the list no longer than half the number of students in your class—if you have 20 students, list 10 animals. For each animal, make two name tags in the shape of that animal. On the back of each name tag write that animal's name.

Give a name tag to each student. Each student looks at the name on her name tag (keeping it a secret). When you say "Go," have each student make the appropriate sound for the animal on her name tag. Then each student finds the other student who is making the same sound. Ask each pair to sit, facing one another.

Give each pair the following list of prompts to discuss together:

1. Which animal do you think you are most like and why?

2. Think about your family members and decide which animal each one is like and why.

3. If you had the chance to be any animal in the world for one day, which would you choose and why?

Answering these questions will build a classroom community by helping students express themselves and learn about their classmates.

Celebrate with animal crackers!

STRATEGY 23

Appreciation Circle

Have students form a circle with their arms around each other's waists. Ask them to take small steps to the left as you play slow, reflective music. Explain that you will continue to let the music play until a student says, "I appreciate..." Stop the music, and that student then shares an appreciation about another student, the class, or you, the teacher.

When the student is finished, start the music again. Students take small steps to the right until someone else says, "I appreciate..."

Continue this until you think the class is through and then say, "Appreciations going once, going twice..." If no one responds with a final appreciation, thank the class for their comments and give them an appreciation from you.

We are very good at saying things we don't like about someone else. Having students take time to appreciate others helps create a safe and caring classroom community.

ANOTHER WAY

Sometimes students become distracted by the music and activity while waiting for their turns. As an alternative, play background music while giving students quiet time at their desks for reflection. As the music plays softly, have students write down or record what they want to say. Then share the notes of appreciation in class.

STRATEGY 24

Praise Behind Your Back

Explain to students that a class norm will be that if they talk about someone else behind his back, the comments need to be positive. This activity helps them learn this norm.

One student sits in a chair with his back to the rest of the class. That student brings paper and a pencil with him to the chair.

When you give the signal, the other students in the class have one minute to say positive things about the student sitting in the chair. Meanwhile, that student writes down all the positive things the other students say during the minute. In this way, students talk positively about a classmate behind his back.

Keep students' names in a jar and select them randomly, making sure every student has a chance to sit in the chair by the end of the school year.

STRATEGY 25

Resident Experts

The purpose of this activity is to create a classroom environment in which students seek out each other's help. Each student becomes a class expert who helps classmates with academic or nonacademic tasks. Students design and post business cards to let others know their areas of expertise. (See examples below.)

Bring in a variety of business cards to share with the class. Have them identify the purposes of the various cards and notice their unique logos and features.

Give each student a sheet of blank paper and a blank 3" × 5" index card. (Younger students can use larger cards.)

Ask students to identify their own strengths in areas such as math, spelling, art, music, vocabulary, sports, identifying bugs, map reading, and so on. Students take their lists to you so you can make a final selection.

Once you and the student agree on her area of expertise, the student designs and creates a business card that will notify others of how and when she can help.

To support this strategy, think of each person in your class, identify one or more strengths that student possesses, and create an appropriate business card for her. In the event a student says to you, "I can't do anything!", hand the student a pre-made card identifying her strengths.

The business cards can be posted at centers or stored in folders or photograph albums.

STRATEGY 26

Clock Partners

Give each student a clock face (see reproducible in the Appendix on page 127). Each student puts his name on his clock face and then finds other students to be his clock partners. He makes appointments with a different partner for each hour on the clock face.

Periodically ask students to meet with a clock partner to discuss any content in which students are engaged. For example, ask students to meet with their 10 o'clock partners to discuss a favorite character from a book they are studying.

If you find students are meeting only with their best friends, request they sign up close friends on the first few hours on their clocks and sign up students they don't know as well on the lines for later hours. This is a way to get your students to work with students they don't normally interact with.

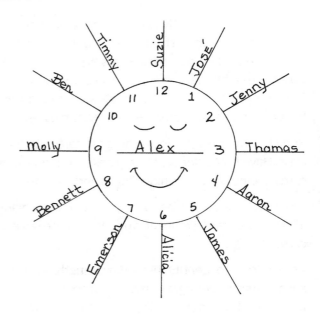

STRATEGY 27

Mix It, Mix It

Students walk around the room saying, "Mix it, mix it."

Tell students that you will say several food names. When they hear one they like, they flock together. Example: As students are walking around, say, "Ice Cream, Apples, Pizza, Chicken." You could also call out a category like "Pizza" and then have students identify different kinds of pizza and group themselves by pizza toppings (e.g., cheese with pepperoni). Then ask each group to tell the rest of the class what toppings its pizza has.

This activity promotes interaction and cooperation as students get acquainted.

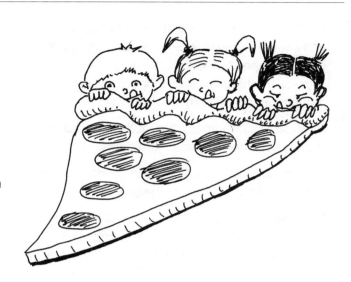

STRATEGY 28

Toothpaste

For this activity you need a tube of toothpaste and a sheet of paper. Squeeze a little toothpaste onto the paper. Ask several students to also squeeze toothpaste onto the paper. You can walk around the room as you are doing this.

Now ask a student to put the toothpaste back into the tube. Repeat with several students.

Ask the students, "Would we ever be able to get all the toothpaste back into the tube?"

When students say "No," say, "It is just like that with the words we use with one another. Our words last a long, long time. There will always be a residue. Therefore, we should be careful that our words we use with one another are helpful and not hurtful."

This activity sends a very visual message of the importance of respectful communication.

STRATEGY 29

We're Going on a Scavenger Hunt!

This is a getting-to-know-you activity that helps students identify their interests as they relate to what we know about multiple intelligences.

Photocopy the Multiple Intelligence Scavenger Hunt reproducible in the Appendix on page 128.

Give each student a copy. Tell the class that each student is to interview all the other students in the class, asking them to initial every item that relates to them.

When the class is ready, discuss what they have discovered about each other. You might graph the different interests or strengths.

Collect the scavenger-hunt sheets when the activity is finished. The information they contain will help you discover the strengths of all of your students.

ANOTHER WAY

Help bodily-kinesthetic learners apply their strengths appropriately. Provide many opportunities for them to demonstrate a process or a technology, give a recital or audition, make models, run errands, create visuals, lead an expedition, and so on. Track their progress and celebrate their successes, while encouraging them to explore new ways to learn.

STRATEGY 30

Blindfold

Put a blindfold on each student.

After the blindfolds are in place, ask the students to line up according to their height, tallest to shortest, without talking.

Process this activity by asking the following questions:

1. How did you feel while participating in this activity?

2. What did you learn from this activity?

Guide students to the understanding that they needed one another to complete this activity. In a caring classroom, we all need one another.

Another approach is to skip the blindfolds. Ask students to line up, without talking, according to the month and day of each student's birthday.

STRATEGY 31

Flying High with Praise

Give each student a sheet of paper.

Each student writes his name on the paper and folds the paper into an airplane.

Play some music while students fly their papers around the room.

When the music stops, each student picks up the airplane that is closest to him and writes a positive comment about the student whose name is on the plane.

Play the music again so the students can send the messages to the intended recipients. Give students time to enjoy their messages!

STRATEGY 32

The Classroom Buzz

Have students work in pairs. Each partner takes a turn answering the questions on the Buzz Sheet. (See reproducible in the Appendix on page 129.)

For added fun, have students switch partners for each section of the handout.

This quick mixer activity involves students with light questions that can lead to deeper insight. Students have the opportunity to get acquainted and, perhaps, see a different side of their peers. You can also replace the Buzz Sheet with test questions or have students create their own Buzz Sheet items.

STRATEGY 33

The One and Only Me

Give each student paper and a pencil. Explain that each student should write an advertisement for someone to replace her. She should list the qualities that she feels are most important. Suggest students include things they like to do; things they don't like to do; a special place they have always wanted to visit; favorite subject, food, sport, color; and so on.

Model this activity for them by writing on the board an advertisement for yourself. For example, you might write:

WANTED: Someone to be Mrs. Jones for a day. Must love to teach, especially third graders. Must collect stuffed animals, like to dance, and enjoy reading good books.

After the students write their advertisements, place them all in a paper bag. Have each student pick one and read it aloud to the rest of the class. The class tries to guess who the person is.

ANOTHER WAY

Have students prepare questions and interview family members for information to include in their ads. Families are good resources for identifying strengths and sharing insights that build students' self-esteem and confidence. Assist students in illustrating the ideas in the ads.

STRATEGY 34

Well, I Never!

You will need between 15 and 30 pieces of string per student (depending on how long you want the game to last).

Give each student 15 to 30 pieces of string and have everyone sit in a circle. One person begins by saying, "I have never..." and completes the sentence by saying something he has never done. Everyone who has done what the speaker has never done gives the speaker a piece of string. If no one in the circle has done it, the speaker gives each player a piece of string. The "winner" is the one with the most pieces of string.

The game's strategy is for students to say something they have never done but think many of their classmates have done. Example: "I have never been on a soccer team." Since many students have played soccer on a team, the student making this statement would receive many strings.

This fun, get-acquainted game is a great way to identify common interests as well as unique traits among your students. An added benefit is the fact that students must think of strategies to win this game.

STRATEGY 35

Power Up Your Center Time

Utilizing the interactive whiteboard as a learning center for small groups allows more students to interact with the board and enables you to tier lessons easily.

Search online and choose from a number of high-quality, interactive whiteboard lessons that align with your objectives and accommodate students' readiness levels. Look for activities that are eye-catching and game-like, and make sure they provide immediate feedback to support student self-reflection and enrich understanding.

To use activities for independent work, save your favorite interactive whiteboard lessons to the computer desktop. Doing so provides learners with a visual icon they can easily find and use on their own. You can even manage the rotation of students among centers by using a timer from the resources in your interactive whiteboard software.

Websites for Interactive Whiteboard Resources

ABCYA: abcya.com
Educational games and apps

eThemes: ethemes.missouri.edu
Kid-safe online resources

SMART Exchange: exchange.smarttech.com
Ready-to-use SMART Board lessons

Promethean Planet: prometheanplanet.com
ActivBoard lessons

STRATEGY 36

Talk to Yourself

Students who have difficulty discriminating among different phonemes can be helped with the phonics phone. When a student speaks into the phonics phone, the sound is immediately repeated back to her. This instant feedback assists the student in making the correct sound as spoken by the teacher or mentor.

Phonics phones are also useful for older students. Have them whisper-read when revising and editing their work.

To assemble a phonics phone, attach two two-inch-diameter PVC plastic elbows onto a two-inch-diameter PVC plastic coupling.

Materials

PVC plastic parts are available from most hardware stores.

Ready-made phonics phones are available from:

Crystal Springs Books
10 Sharon Road
P.O. Box 500
Peterborough, NH 03458
1-800-321-0401
SDE.com/crystalsprings

Twist and Learn with Wikki Stix

Wikki Stix are hands-on teaching tools made from wax. Resembling pieces of colored yarn, they bend into different shapes and easily stick to each other and to other surfaces. They also come apart easily and leave no marks or residue. They are excellent tools for your tactile or kinesthetic learners to use in a variety of ways.

Students can form letters, numbers, and shapes from Wikki Stix.

Art, science, social-studies, and other academic-area projects can be made from Wikki Stix.

They are great materials to have at your learning centers.

Materials

Wikki Stix are available from many teacher-supply stores and from:

Crystal Springs Books
10 Sharon Road
P.O. Box 500
Peterborough, NH 03458
1-800-321-0401
SDE.com/crystalsprings

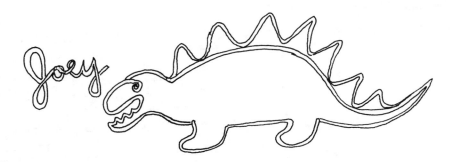

STRATEGY 38

You Can Count on Bingo Chips

Many math manipulative kits include colored, transparent plastic counters. Instead of using these, try working with magnetic bingo chips.

"Magnetic" bingo chips are similar to other math counters, except each one has a metal rim around the circumference, so the chips can be picked up by magnets. Students can use them in counting activities or to search for patterns on number charts. They are effective manipulatives, and they are easily collected with magnets or magnetic wands after students complete an activity.

A great "sponge activity" for early finishers can be looking for numerical patterns on a Hundreds Chart. Have students use bingo chips to highlight each pattern they discover!

See the reproducible for a Hundreds Chart in the Appendix on page 130.

Materials

Bingo chips can be purchased at teacher stores, online, or through math catalogs.

Hundreds Chart

1	2	3	4	5	6	7	8	9	10
11	12	13	14	15	16	17	18	19	20
21	22	23	24	25	26	27	28	29	30
31	32	33	34	35	36	37	38	39	40
41	42	43	44	45	46	47	48	49	50
51	52	53	54	55	56	57	58	59	60
61	62	63	64	65	66	67	68	69	70
71	72	73	74	75	76	77	78	79	80
81	82	83	84	85	86	87	88	89	90
91	92	93	94	95	96	97	98	99	100

STRATEGY **39**

Let the Games Begin

We know that getting students moving can boost learning. Addressing each of the learning modalities is necessary for true differentiation. And ongoing assessment guides us in planning lessons and selecting grouping strategies. One way to accomplish all of the above is game playing, which allows you to involve all learners and check for understanding at the same time.

The whole group can benefit by playing games you create from PowerPoint templates or find on interactive websites and show with an LCD projector. Small groups can play review or enrichment games on the interactive whiteboard while you are coaching other students. And individuals can play educational games on the computer or on mobile devices as anchor activities to perfect their skills. Interactive games are ideal for differentiation because they can accommodate a broad range of interests, learning styles, and skill levels.

Be sure to structure the game playing so that both you and your students can assess results. For example, consider having students keep game journals in which they set goals, record scores, and reflect on their progress. Analyze the data periodically to inform instruction and remediation.

Online PowerPoint Games and Templates

people.uncw.edu/ertzbergerj/ppt_games.html

jc-schools.net/tutorials/ppt-games

Free Game Sites for Students

ABCYA: abcya.com
Educational computer games and activities

PBS Kids: pbskids.org/whiteboard
Interactive whiteboard games

Manga High: mangahigh.com/en_us
Free math games for K–12

Math Snacks: mathsnacks.org
Mini math games

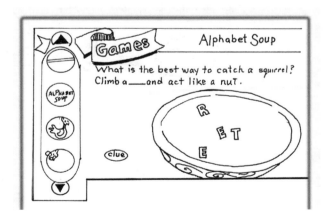

STRATEGY **40**

Funneling Information

Create a "talking tube" similar to the ones used on early ships for communication between decks.

Construction is easy: Simply attach a medium-size plastic funnel to each end of a four-foot-long, one-half-inch-diameter plastic tube. This device allows students to work quietly together without disturbing their neighbors.

This is a great tool for English language learners who need the support of a nearby student interpreter.

ANOTHER WAY

Make a list of the domain-specific vocabulary your English language learners need to know and distribute the list for easy reference. Have students look up the words, their meanings, and pronunciations in print and online resources. Use this strategy for multiple-meaning words, idioms, and figurative language, too. (See merriam-webster.com.)

Vocal Immersion

Try vocal immersion: When parallel reading with your students, use an old stethoscope or a nonelectrical-style airplane headphone. Cup the tube end in your hand while directing your voice into the tube as you read.

Extraneous classroom noises are blocked out, and the student hears precision speaking as the teacher reads the passage.

This is a helpful technique for students who have attention problems and for those with difficulty distinguishing sounds.

STRATEGY **42**

There's an App for That

When purchasing new technology for the classroom, consider iPads, netbooks, and iPods. These wireless devices are less expensive than traditional desktop computers with Internet access, and they allow students to conduct web-based research, listen to podcasts, watch videos, and play games that reinforce learning. Many educational applications provide immediate feedback so students can monitor their own progress.

Because they have no cables or cords, mobile devices also allow you the flexibility to change the arrangement of your classroom. You can reconfigure your small groups as often as necessary to meet the needs of different lessons and different students. You can also personalize instruction by selecting apps that align to specific student needs.

Online Sources for Applications

Apple: apple.com/education/apps

Fun Educational Apps: funeducationalapps.com

AppShopper: appshopper.com

STRATEGY 43

Highlighting What's Important

Highlighting tape is colored transparent tape that comes in different widths, including full sheets; can be placed over print; and is reusable.

Highlighting tape helps students find information and focus on skills in all academic areas. Young students can use the wide tape during interactive writing and when working with charts. They can also use it to find and highlight letters or words that are the focus of instruction.

Older students can use narrow highlighting tape in novels to identify parts of speech, new vocabulary words, and answers to comprehension questions.

Highlighting tape not only helps students focus on learning but is also an excellent alternative form of responding. Students with fine-motor difficulties especially like the opportunity to show what they know by highlighting their answers instead of always having to write them on paper.

Materials

Highlighting tape is available from many teacher-supply stores and from:

Crystal Springs Books
10 Sharon Road
P.O. Box 500
Peterborough, NH 03458
1-800-321-0401
SDE.com/crystalsprings

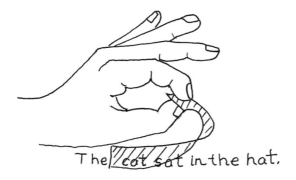

The cat sat in the hat.

ANOTHER WAY

Some students may get carried away and highlight everything that looks important in a block of text. Teach them not to highlight titles, headings, and words that appear in boldface. Demonstrate how to find and support key ideas in text so that students use highlighting to inform and organize their note taking.

STRATEGY 44

"Post It" with Notes

Post-it Notes are versatile teaching tools students can use to respond to text and focus on specific problems or parts of a page.

Focusing tool. Students who are overwhelmed with an entire page of math problems can use Post-it Notes to focus their attention on the problem at hand. The child surrounds or frames the math problem with Post-it Notes. Also, with an addition problem involving numbers in the hundreds, the student can use a small Post-it Note to cover the hundreds and tens places so she can focus on adding the units. Next, the child uncovers the tens place, and finally the hundreds place. This step-by-step process reinforces place value and helps prevent errors.

Responding to text. Post-it Notes are excellent for finding and marking text responses when students are working individually or in a small or large group. They can also be used to locate and prove an answer, write text-to-text or text-to-self notes, and "Guess the Hidden Word."

Revising or editing writing. Students can write revision ideas or editing corrections on Post-it Notes and then put them on their manuscripts for later correction on the computer. Teachers can use Post-it Notes to write notes to students without marking their papers.

Grades or comments can also be written on Post-it Notes and attached at the end of a paper or assignment. There is no permanent mark on the student's work, and privacy is maintained.

Can You Spot the Learning?

Small plastic ants or other insects are highly motivating and practical focusing tools. Introduce the class to "Spot" (or another name of your choice) and describe how Spot can help them in their daily work.

"Spot, the focused ant" covers the digits in the tens and hundreds places while the student adds the units. Spot then moves to the left as the student adds the tens, and then the hundreds.

"Spot, the word-finding ant" can also cover parts of speech, vocabulary words, or other one-word responses. Spot is a great cover-up agent for use in "Guess the Covered Word."

"Spot, the world traveler" loves to mark cities or countries on maps.

Students will love to create new jobs and titles for Spot.

Materials

Plastic insects can be found at most party stores.

STRATEGY 46

Using a Focus Frame to Get the Picture

This easy-to-make tool helps students slide words, sentences, or problems into focus, eliminating other potentially distracting text or pictures from the student's view.

A pattern for a focus frame is included in the Appendix on page 131. Old manila folders provide great material for making the frames. (Creating focus frames is a good task for students to complete at a job center.)

You can make focus frames in a variety of shapes and sizes: small ones for isolating words; long, horizontal ones for reading sentences; and large square ones for working on math problems or reading paragraphs.

Focus frames are excellent tools for helping students focus on one item at a time during testing because they narrow the amount of information that can be seen at one time.

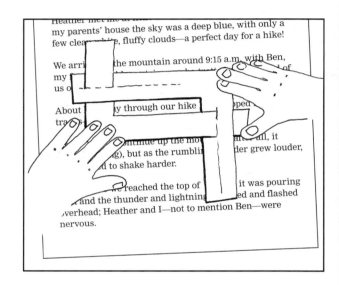

Sliding Mask

Use a sliding mask to help bring focus to words and phrases by blocking out surrounding print. The sliding mask is a handy device to teach students left-to-right flow while reading or to break down words (e.g., prefixes, suffixes, compound words, and syllables).

Try taping a colored strip of transparent plastic to the back of the window of the sliding mask to help those students who experience visual difficulty with black print on white paper.

See page 132 in the Appendix for directions on how to make a Sliding Mask and a pattern for making this easy-to-use device.

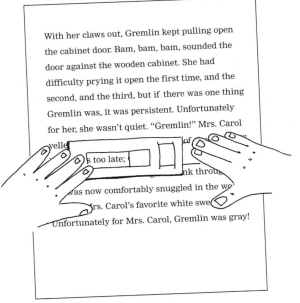

STRATEGY 48

Point the Finger

Use a finger pointer to signal students non-verbally. This is a great way to manage students in a humorous manner without making verbal requests.

The finger pointer is handy for pointing to information on a whiteboard or chart without blocking the students' view. This unusual way to get the attention of your students can be enhanced by the addition of a bulb horn or a bicycle bell.

Materials

Materials for making a finger pointer are readily available. They include:

- An old glove and stuffing
- Wooden dowel (36 inches long with a one-half-inch diameter)
- Glue/adhesive
- Glitter/jewels for rings and decoration (optional)
- Bulb horn or bicycle bell (optional)

STRATEGY 49

Catch That Word

Take words in and out of context with a word catcher. This simple teaching tool allows teachers or students to isolate and bring focus to a specific word. This is an ideal tool for students with attention problems.

To make a word catcher, glue a 4" to 6" piece of white tagboard or thin plastic to the palm side of an old glove. Turn on the LCD projector and stand to one side, halfway between the screen and the projector. Hold the word catcher between the screen and the beam of light from the projector and move the word catcher back and forth until the word comes into focus. The word catcher on your hand will act as a miniature portable screen as you reach out and "snag" a word to bring it out of context to be worked on. When you remove your hand, the word goes back into context.

Note: A white cutting board can also work well as a word catcher.

Materials

- Old glove
- 4" to 6" piece of tagboard or plastic
- Adhesive or glue

STRATEGY 50

In Praise of Page Protectors

Page protectors offer an alternate way of writing answers on work sheets or activity sheets.

Students slide a work sheet or a photocopy of an assignment into a page protector, then write the answers on the acetate with a dry-erase marker. They can use rags, socks, or tissues to erase and clean up.

Page protectors help save paper, particularly if you do math-fact practice every day. Students can respond, correct, and erase instead of responding, correcting, and then throwing away.

Students love using page protectors as a break from typical paper-and-pencil tasks. After you or the student corrects the page, it is simply erased and ready for use again. The work sheet is stored for future use.

Page protectors at learning centers provide an opportunity for students to work on different activity sheets or portable centers, correct their answers, erase, and return the sheets or centers for another student to use.

A variety of colored page protectors can be helpful for those students who have difficulty with black-on-white contrast.

STRATEGY **51**

Get a Grip on It

Many students have poor handwriting skills due to fine-motor problems caused by incorrect initial instruction. Some students are encouraged to write too early or are forced to write cursively before they are developmentally ready. (We strongly recommend not teaching cursive until students are around eight years old.)

Try using a variety of pencil grips to improve the student's grasp. We suggest form-fitting pens and pencils. Many schools have great success with Hand Huggers, triangle-shaped pencils that are easily grasped by students with handwriting difficulties. Hand Huggers fit standard classroom pencil sharpeners with adjustable openings. They are also a viable alternative for older students who may resist using a pencil grip.

Materials

Handwriting tools are available online and from most teacher-supply stores.

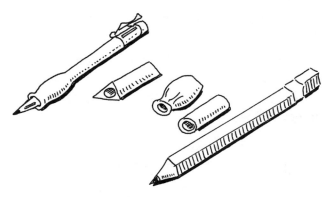

STRATEGY 52

Watch and Learn

It is difficult to find tools that appeal to all learners, but video is one of those resources. By strategically placing video clips in your instruction, you can increase interest as you introduce a concept, review material, or extend a previous lesson. The best video clips vividly show or teach an idea and run no more than five minutes. Search online to find videos that capture student attention and make them think. Be sure to include time for discussion or written reflections after viewing, and make the videos available to students to watch again as needed.

Take time to post links to the selected videos to an email, newsletter, or class website. Encourage parents to view the videos too as a resource for homework help.

Online Sources for Educational Videos

BrainPOP: brainpop.com
Animated videos and games

Khan Academy: khanacademy.org
Extensive library of tutorials

PBS LearningMedia: pbslearningmedia.org
Video library

Science Kids: sciencekids.co.nz
Science experiments, games, projects, and videos

WatchKnowLearn: watchknowlearn.org
Educational videos for K–12

ANOTHER WAY

Consider using video prior to your instruction. Have students watch a video as homework or as an introduction to a concept, and then use class time to provide instruction based on differing student skill levels. For example, a homework assignment might require students to watch a student-friendly video about how sound works. When students return to class, you would have them complete a simple assessment based on the video. Depending on the results, you would assign each student to work on one of several sound experiments you have prepared. This is called flipping the class.

STRATEGY 53

It's About Time

Often students from low-income families are not in sync with the time orientation required by the school and workplace. The school is often the only place where a student is taught the importance of "school time" orientation.

Try using three-, four-, and five-minute sand timers as a way to help students visualize time as both finite and fleeting. To help students quicken their work pace, challenge them to beat a timer as they solve math problems.

The following represent some of the hallmarks of time orientation in poverty:

- Time is neither measured nor heeded.

- Time is thought of only in the present; plans for the future seldom exist.

- The rate of absenteeism is high.

- The student is often a late arrival or a no-show.

- The student has difficulty with delaying gratification.

- Projects and tasks are not completed in a timely fashion.

- The student has a tendency to be reactive rather than proactive.

- The work pace is slow.

Note: These hallmarks are typical of a pattern. All patterns have exceptions.

STRATEGY 54

Memorize with Mnemonics

A mnemonic device is a memory trigger or reminder, like a sticky note on a page. People often generate simple mnemonics to help them remember a list or the steps in a process. For example, the word c-a-t can remind a shopper to buy crackers, apples, and tea.

The brain seeks meaning, so associating new concepts with words, acronyms, poems, pictures, or songs helps students to remember needed information. Students with different learning styles respond to different mnemonic devices. Encourage students to try out a variety and use the ones that work best for them. Here are a few simple examples to get them thinking.

- Acronyms: H-O-M-E-S for the Great Lakes (Huron, Ontario, Michigan, Erie, and Superior).

- Buried Letters: Stala<u>c</u>tites hang from the roof or "ceiling" of a cave, while stalagmites grow from deposits on the ground.

- Embedded Definitions: Ride the outer <u>rim</u> to find pe<u>rim</u>eter. <u>Cir</u>cle round the middle to find <u>cir</u>cumference.

- Jingles: Sing the letters of a new six-letter word to the tune of "Happy Birthday to You." Sing the letters of a new seven-letter word to the tune of "Twinkle, Twinkle, Little Star."

- Rhyme: Thirty days hath September, April, June, and November.

STRATEGY 55

Quiet, Please!
Student at Work

It is not that a student with attention problems can't pay attention; it is that she does pay attention—to every sound. That is the student's downfall.

Provide easily distracted students with noise-suppressing ear protection. This will block out extraneous distracting sounds that take them off-task.

Materials

Noise-suppressing ear-protection devices are available from most hardware stores.

To help struggling students get more out of study time, brainstorm with them a list of obstacles to learning; the list might include noise, disorganization, and interruptions. Then demonstrate practical ideas for overcoming these obstacles, such as posting a Quiet Zone sign on the door, gathering study materials ahead of time, and turning off cell phones and iPods.

STRATEGY 56

Enlarge Print and Eliminate Distracting Artwork

Use a photocopier to enlarge the print for students who have difficulty focusing when reading small print.

Try eliminating distracting designs and artwork for students who are visually "led astray" by non-essential artwork on a page.

Large print also makes it easier to use highlighting tape, which can further enhance focusing.

Georgie Porgie, pudding and pie.
Kissed the girls and made them cry;
When the girls came out to play,
Georgie Porgie ran away.

gie Porgie, pudding and pie.
ed the girls and made them cry;
h the girls came out to play,
gie Porgie ran away.

Lights, Camera, Writing

Even the most reluctant writer is drawn to the idea of being part of movie production. Tap into that enthusiasm by using Internet resources to make a class movie or slide show based on content the class is studying. Assign students to a variety of roles: writers, director, and so on. You get to differentiate based on learning styles and interests, and students are strongly motivated because they take ownership of their learning. At the same time, you're building comprehension and fluency through the repetition and practice involved in the project.

To build confidence and instill a feeling of success, be sure to share the final product with a real audience.

Multi-media Production and Presentation Websites

Animoto: animoto.com/education

Smilebox: smilebox.com

Movie Maker (for Windows-based computers): explore.live.com/windows-live-movie-maker

iMovie (for Macs): apple.com/support/imovie/

STRATEGY 58

Familiarity Breeds Attempt

Pre-teach new or difficult concepts as a strategy to reduce the anxiety and stress often experienced by discouraged learners when new or challenging material or concepts are introduced.

When struggling students are given a preview of things to come, it enhances their confidence while building a can-do attitude. Pre-teaching is also an excellent way to activate prior knowledge, an important first step in engaging learners.

When previewing new material for struggling students, group related ideas together. For example, the illustration lists separate writing conventions, but together they form an editing checklist. By providing the context, you help students build on prior knowledge and make valuable connections.

STRATEGY 59

Bring It into Focus

When students with Scotopic Sensitivity Syndrome read black print on white paper, the print appears to shake, letters appear reversed, and the print may seem out of focus.

Researchers have found that when you place frosted colored overlays on top of the print, visual distortions are dramatically reduced.

These high-quality overlays come in eight different colors. Different students seem to benefit from using different colors. (A particular color that works for one student may not work for another.)

Sample test questions include:

- Do you skip words or lines when reading?
- Do you need to take breaks often?
- Do you find it harder to read the longer you read?
- Do you get headaches when you read?
- Do your eyes get red and watery when you read?
- Do you read with your face close to the page?

For more questions, see the reproducible test for Scotopic Sensitivity Syndrome in the Appendix on page 133.

More Information on Scotopic Sensitivity Syndrome

The Irlen Institute
5380 Village Road
Long Beach, CA 90808
1-800-55-IRLEN
irlen.com

Materials

Frosted color overlays and *Reading by the Colors* by Helen L. Irlen are available from the Irlen Institute.

Adapted with permission from *Reading by the Colors* by Helen L. Irlen, Penguin Putnam/Perigee Div. Publishers.

STRATEGY 60

Human Scrabble

Make two sets of letters of the alphabet on small squares of paper. Each set (one for each team) should be on a different color of paper.

Divide the class into two teams. Each team member should receive some of the letters to spread out on his/her desk.

Pose a question, such as how to spell a word, a question related to content, etc.

Students look to see if they have a letter contained in the answer. If they do, they pick it up and quickly go the front of the room. The team that has the correct answer first wins.

STRATEGY **61**

Ready, Set, Create!

To develop higher-order thinking skills and deepen understanding, try having students create digital comic strips as an after-reading activity in any content area. Doing so requires them to develop a new product based on the information they have been given— calling on them to use creativity, one of the highest levels of thinking.

Educational websites provide the tools and templates students can use to make and animate their own creations. Whether they create a single frame or an entire strip, in the process learners must analyze, synthesize, and evaluate information they've gleaned from their reading. Even students who don't think of themselves as artists can succeed with digital comics, and it's easy to differentiate because each student can read text appropriate for her level.

Once students have developed their comics, display those creations in your resource center or library. Together discuss other options for publishing student work, such as posting the comics to your school's website or including them in your class newsletter.

Websites for Creating Comics

Comic Master: comicmaster.org.uk

Creaza Education: creazaeducation.com

NCTE Read Write Think: readwritethink.org/files/ resources/interactives/comic

Professor Garfield: professorgarfield.org/ starsleeper/comiccreator.html

STRATEGY 62

Finding Your Voice

Improve comprehension for all learning styles by showing your enthusiasm in a variety of ways when reading aloud. Vary your pacing, sounds, animation, tone of voice, volume, facial expressions, hand gestures, and so on. Encourage students to do the same with their own oral reading.

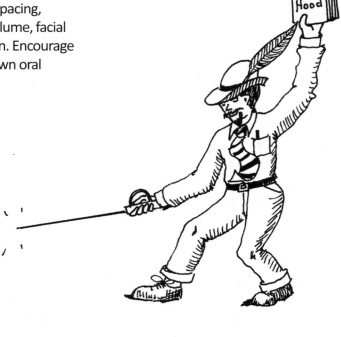

Take this activity one step further by having students who are comfortable in front of an audience actually perform favorite lines from stories they have read and enjoyed. Alternatively, assign teams. Some students can write stage directions for performing favorite lines, and others can follow those directions and deliver the lines.

STRATEGY **63**

First Things First: Cross the Midline

Some students experience reading and writing difficulty due to an inability to cross the brain's midline (i.e., the body's center meridian).

When reading and/or writing, these students might hesitate or stop in the center of the page. Some students may actually start over again or go to the next line without completing the current line.

The left and right hemispheres often don't interact efficiently until students are around six years of age. This can pose a problem for developmentally young children who are being required to "sweep their eyes" from left to right before they are physiologically ready to do so.

To determine whether a student is able to cross the midline, simply have her reach up over her head and cup and hold the opposite ear. This is a difficult task for those with difficulty crossing the midline. Another test calls for having a student draw a large circle on the whiteboard in one motion. If a child moves the marker from one hand to another halfway through or takes a side step to complete the circle, she might have midline problems.

If a child is fully six years old and still experiencing difficulty crossing the midline, help may be warranted.

Occupational therapists suggest the following:

- Have the student draw an imaginary figure eight in the air. Do this eight to ten times, alternating hands.

- Reach across with one hand and touch the opposite thigh or knee. Do this eight to ten times, alternating hands.

- Have the student lift her leg, reach back with the opposite hand, and touch the raised heel. Do this six to eight times, alternating hands each time.

STRATEGY **64**

Teach in Chunks

"Can't see the forest for the trees" is one way to describe the confusion felt by some students who are bewildered by an overly integrated curriculum. When several subjects or concepts are blended together in an integrated format, some students experience information overload.

These students might learn some concepts best when the concepts are presented in meaningful, bite-size chunks. For these students, learning the parts to the whole makes the most sense.

ANOTHER WAY

Help bodily-kinesthetic learners learn and apply complex concepts or processes through word play and visualization. Acronyms, simple rhymes, tongue twisters, jingles, comic strips, and story boards can help to break down complex concepts into manageable chunks.

STRATEGY 65
Digital R.A.F.T.

R.A.F.T., the acronym for Role, Audience, Format, and Topic, is a strategy that gets students to write from perspectives other than their own. Each student takes on a persona, such as a favorite character or a famous person; chooses an audience; selects a genre for his topic, such as a letter, a speech, or a poem; and determines which topic he wants to focus on. Provide students with a chart of possible R.A.F.T. options, and differentiate by allowing each learner to choose one option from each category and create a finished product based on that selection.

Differentiate even more and increase enthusiasm by offering students web-based options for presenting their work. They can use web-based avatars to deliver their writing, create a video using Little Bird Tales, or display their work electronically using Voice Thread.

Web-Based Presentation Tools

Voki: voki.com
Avatars

FlipSnack: flipsnack.com
Flipbook creator

Little Bird Tales: littlebirdtales.com
Narration of own stories

Voice Thread: ed.voicethread.com
Displaying and commenting on presentations

Role	Audience	Format	Topic
Wolf	Rabbits	Voki avatar	Carnivore/herbivore relationship
Marc Brown (author)	Arthur (book character)	FlipSnack	Future storylines
News Reporter	Public	Little Bird Tales or Voice Thread	History of the community

STRATEGY 66

C.A.P.S. Off to Editing

This mnemonic management process for editing helps students check their conventions in writing, one step at a time.

Start with four baseball caps, each a different color. On the rim of each, write the first letter of one of the following cues: Capitalization, Agreement, Punctuation, or Spelling.

Hang four hooks at your writing center and hang the caps on them.

Make up four checklists for students to easily reference while they edit. The first checklist should have examples of capitalization rules that you have studied to date. The second should list rules for subject/verb agreement; the third, punctuation; and the fourth, spelling. Laminate the checklists or place them in pocket portfolios, and then hang each on a hook below the corresponding cap.

Explain to students that they are to edit their writing by focusing on one area at a time, beginning with the C for capitalization and continuing until they have spelled C.A.P.S.

STRATEGY 67

Word Clouds

Word clouds visually represent and organize key concepts in colorful and engaging formats. Somewhat like shape poems, word clouds focus the eyes on important vocabulary through the use of color, alignment, and shape.

Go to Wordle.net or Tagxedo.com to create a word cloud for free. Then, to introduce vocabulary prior to reading text, ask students to examine your creation, looking for familiar terms and unknown words. You can also set a purpose for reading and heighten interest in the subject matter by having students work from a word cloud to make predictions about a story or book before reading it.

Another option is to ask students to create their own word clouds after finishing their reading. Use the results as a summative assessment and a basis for planning future instruction or remediation.

STRATEGY 68

4-6-8

Have students make three columns on a piece of paper.

Instruct them to number the first column one through four and label it "Characters," number the second column one through six and label it "Settings," and number the third column one through eight and label it "Events."

In the first column, students list characters from any books they have read. The characters do not all have to be from the same book.

In the second column, students write different settings where a story could take place.

In the last column, students write different events that could happen in a story.

Ask students to circle certain items—their #2 character, their #5 setting, and their #7 event, for example. Each student then writes a story using her circled character, setting, and event.

Students can share their stories with one another.

You can add novelty to this activity by having students work in groups of three. Give a red dot to one student in each group. Each student with a red dot thinks of a character. Give a blue dot to another student in each group. Each student with a blue dot thinks of a setting. Give a green dot to the third student in each group. That student thinks of an event. After the students write a story together, have the students with red dots, for example, switch groups.

See the reproducible for 4-6-8 in the Appendix on page 134.

#2   #5   #7

STRATEGY **69**

The World at Their Fingertips

Virtual field trips allow viewers to experience other locations and time periods through quality websites. The sites appeal to all learning styles, and you can differentiate your instruction by selecting online field trips that align with your students' interests, readiness, and prior knowledge.

Use virtual field trips before the class reads text or discusses vocabulary; students will be hooked from the very beginning of your instruction. Refer to the field trips throughout the unit or lesson and encourage students to respond through writing, discussion, drawing, or acting.

One of the most popular sites for virtual field trips is Google Earth, which allows students to "fly" to various locations and observe the landscape, buildings, and much more. Create your own tours on Google Earth by marking locations on a map and recording the journey to share with others—or go to the Google Earth Showcase, which has many tours already created and available to use in the classroom. To support your reading instruction, check out Google Lit Trips, which offers virtual field trips based on favorite books.

Virtual Travel Websites

Google Earth: google.com/earth
Digital overviews of specific physical locations

Google Earth Showcase: google.com/earth/explore/showcase
Tours already created by others

Google Lit Trips: googlelittrips.org
Interactive literary experiences

Simple K12: simplek12.com/virtualfieldtrips
Virtual field trips

The Teacher's Guide: theteachersguide.com/virtualtours.html
Virtual tours of museums and exhibits

Utah Education Network: uen.org/tours
Already-created virtual field trips and tools for creating your own

STRATEGY 70

Word Map

Divide students into teams.

Give each team a large sheet of paper and some markers.

Assign to each team a different vocabulary word or concept being studied.

Each team should create a Word Map using the reproducible guide in the Appendix on page 135.

Maps can be presented to the rest of the class and hung in the classroom.

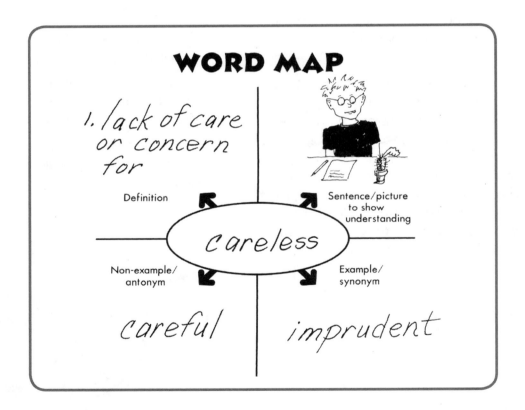

STRATEGY 71

Three Facts
and a Fib

Give each student an index card. Ask students to make up four statements about any content they have studied. Three of the statements should be true, and one should be false.

Students then move around the room sharing statements with one another. Students try to pick the false statement on each card. If a student fools another student, the student who was fooled signs the back of the index card of the student who fooled him.

After students have returned to their seats, have them count the signatures on the backs of their cards. The person who was able to fool the most students is the winner.

ANOTHER WAY

To help students prepare for tests, create "Facts and Fib" card sets for your study center or class website. Then have study partners select a set of cards from the collection, locate the facts in their own notes, and correct the fibs. Remind them to verify their corrections and cite their sources.

STRATEGY 72

Splash and Sort

Attract student attention and interest by "splashing" words from a reading selection at angles and projecting them with a document camera before students have read the selection.

In teams, students work to create one or more sentences combining some or all of the words. This requires them to predict how the words might go together in the text they are about to read.

After the class has read the material, each group can discuss their predictions and modify their statements considering the new information they have.

Another way for students to use the Splash and Sort strategy is to work in pairs and categorize words about a particular concept the class is about to study.

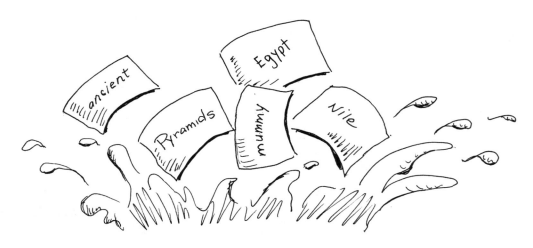

STRATEGY 73

In the News

You can differentiate informational text lessons by offering a variety of both topics and reading levels in the news articles students read. Online news sources can be a great help with this. Providing student choice in the selection of reading materials builds intrinsic motivation for reading.

Have students form literature circles around the types of articles they're reading. Then have them read, analyze, and discuss the text together. Be sure to schedule time for each circle to summarize the information for the class.

You can easily extend your students' learning and build critical thinking skills through reading-related activities. For example, you might invite students to work collaboratively to write songs, poems, and short plays based on their reading. Others may want to design artwork (pictures, posters, cartoons, diagrams) to interpret the text. Still others may choose to promote a cause or organize a community event. Offering a choice of after-reading activities builds intrinsic motivation and opens different pathways to learning.

Online News Sources

TweenTribune: tweentribune.com
High-interest articles for students

Newseum: newseum.org/todaysfrontpages
Current news from many news sources

Newspaper in Education: nieonline.com
Content and web support for Newspaper in Education programs

ANOTHER WAY

To further differentiate instruction, pre-assess students and create reading groups based on reading level and learning style as well as interests.

STRATEGY 74

C.P.S.R. (Copy-Pair-Share-Respond)

After students have read from a chapter book or content area, ask them to copy in a writing journal the part they found most interesting. Tell them to copy the sentences clearly so another student can read them.

Students trade journals with a partner.

Each student reads what her partner has written and then responds in writing. This back-and-forth "conversation" can last as long as you deem necessary.

Peer response through a silent, written conversation is social and motivational.

See the list of C.P.S.R. Starters in the Appendix on page 136. Students can use these if they need support in responding to what their partners have written.

STRATEGY 75

Apply a Different Symbol System

Direct instruction of vocabulary words or concepts should involve more than just looking up the words in the dictionary. For active involvement and deep processing of the words being studied, ask students to do the following:

- Draw the word.

- Act out the word.

- Think of a song title for the word.

Students can pair off and share their drawings, act out their charades for one another, and share song titles.

When you ask students to draw their vocabulary word, you are tapping into their visual/spatial intelligence. When you ask students to act out their word, you are tapping into their bodily/kinesthetic intelligence. When you ask students to think of a song title, you are tapping into their musical intelligence. The chances of students remembering the words are greater because of their active involvement.

ANOTHER WAY

Use multiple intelligence activities to help English language learners reduce the number of spelling errors in writing. For example, tap out four beats for the number 4 to help them remember the word contains four letters, or search online for finger-spelling images and teach students to finger-spell common homophones.

STRATEGY 76
Colorful Questions

Help students remember the categories of questions in Question-Answer-Relationships (Raphael 1982) by color-coding the questions as follows:

- "Right there" questions are green because you can go to the answer in the book/text.

- "Search and find" questions are yellow because you slow down and look in several places for the answer in the book/text.

- "Author and me" questions are red because you stop and look for clues and evidence the author gives you and combine that with what's in your head to figure out the answer.

- "On my own" questions are blue because you don't have to read the text to answer these.

Examples:

Green Questions	Yellow Questions	Red Questions	Blue Questions
Go to the answer.	*Slow down and look for the answer.*	*Stop and look for clues and evidence.*	*Off the track.*
There was a gas shortage, so Charlene rode her bike to work.	Lil went shopping. She bought flowers at the market. Later she went to the hardware store and bought a lock for her luggage. At the pet store she bought a collar for her dog.	In 1782, the Founding Fathers selected the bald eagle as the national bird.	Students are going to begin a two-week unit on friendship. Before the unit starts, the teacher asks:
What did Charlene ride to work?	*What did Lil buy on her shopping trip?*	*Name some of the men who might have been voting on the national bird in 1782.*	*What are the qualities of a good friend?*

STRATEGY 77

Over the Head

Put each of the vocabulary words being studied from a unit on a sentence strip. Staple each strip to make a headband.

Distribute the headbands, instructing the students to each put one on without looking at the word on her headband.

When every student has a headband on, they all get up and move around the room, asking each other questions about the vocabulary words on their heads in an attempt to guess the words. Sample questions might be "What is a synonym for me (the word written on the headband)?" or "What is an essential characteristic of me?"

Give students enough time so that they can figure out their word. Students enjoy the active involvement of this strategy.

STRATEGY 78

Partner Pair

Pair your students by reading level.

During Partner Pair, each student sits with his partner. Both have a copy of the same reading book.

Partner A reads aloud for five minutes to Partner B. Partner B then must paraphrase for Partner A what the section that Partner A read was about.

Students then switch roles. To ensure fluency practice, Partner B rereads the last two pages that Partner A read. Repeated readings help build fluency.

Students can keep their own records.

STRATEGY 79
Pass It On

Select a variety of books for students to examine for future independent reading.

Divide students into groups. Give each group a recording form that has a place for writing the book title and comments.

Each student selects a book, examines it, and then fills out the recording form, writing the title and a few brief comments.

After three minutes, students rotate the books to the right, and the process begins again.

At the end of the cycle, each student has examined each book.

Have students put a star next to the title of each one they might want to read during independent reading time.

STRATEGY 80

Sticky-Note Symbols

Before students begin reading a passage of text, provide them with a supply of sticky notes that they can use to record their responses. Use symbols to help students code the text. The coding might include the following symbols:

! means *This is interesting*.

? means *I am confused*.

• means *I already know this*.

Students should place the sticky notes in the text as they respond to what they are reading.

When students are finished reading, they can discuss their markings and their understanding of the passage with a partner.

This strategy helps students focus and think while they are reading.

Team Windowpane Discussion

This strategy gives students the opportunity to visualize, create a nonlinguistic representation, and collaborate in the learning process.

Ask students to put their heads down on their desks and close their eyes. Read to them from a book. As you read, tell them what you are seeing in your mind as you are reading. Ask them to see in their minds what they hear you say.

Keep reading from the selected text as you ask students to continue creating pictures in their minds of what you are reading. Ask them to tell you what they see.

Students work independently to draw pictures of their favorite scenes that they see in their minds. Windowpaning refers to the drawings the students make of their favorite scenes. Students can share their drawings in small groups.

STRATEGY 82

Digital Scavenger Hunts

Scaffold student learning by providing structure and direction for students working with websites. To help students be successful while reading online resources, supply graphic organizers with clues to guide them through the sites.

You can use these digital scavenger hunts to set a purpose for learning, facilitate reading online for information, and build students' curiosity about a topic. It's easy to differentiate instruction by creating multiple scavenger hunts. All hunts can cover the same topic and even ask similar questions, but each can reference websites at a different reading level.

You can use a simple three-column organizer to prepare a digital scavenger hunt. To focus the search, provide questions about the topic in the first column. In the second column, list appropriate websites for gathering information. Distribute the organizer and ask students to find and fill in the answers.

Be sure to double-check each website you are considering to be sure it contains current, accurate information. As students become more skilled in finding information online, encourage them to follow up on research-related questions that deepen their investigations.

Sample Internet Scavenger Hunt

Topic Questions	Go to	Answers
What is archaeology?	amnh.org/ology	
What does a zoo archaeologist study?	bbc.co.uk/learningzone/clips/ what-can-an-archaeologist-learn- from-animal-teeth/7812.html	
What tools does an archaeologist use?	digonsite.com/drdig/realfaqs.html	

STRATEGY 83
Money Summary

On average, the use of academic games in the classroom is associated with a 20% point gain in student achievement (Marzano, 2010). Money Summary makes an academic game out of finding the main idea in text.

Give students a piece of text to read. Explain that as they read the material, they are to list the key words and phrases that convey the main idea. Then each student is to use the words and phrases from his list to write a "Money Summary" with a total value assigned by you. Each word or phrase is worth 10 cents, so if you ask for a $2.00 summary, each student must decide which 20 words or phrases—no more and no less—are most important; those are the ones she must use in her summary.

Have students share their summaries as appropriate.

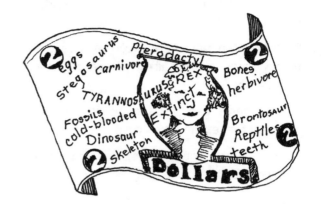

ANOTHER WAY

Differentiate the Money Summary by changing the value you assign. For example, you might ask students to write a $3.50 Money Summary, which would include 35 key words or phrases.

STRATEGY 84

Magic 20

Select a writing passage three to five paragraphs long from material the students are currently reading.

With a document camera, project an image of that passage, covering all the paragraphs except the first one.

Have students read the paragraph in their own copies of the text and then cover it.

Ask students to write a summary from recall in 20 or fewer words.

Repeat this process with the remaining paragraphs.

When the students have summarized all the paragraphs, ask them to combine each pair of summaries in turn, always aiming for a new 20-word summary that covers more and more material. In the end, each student should have one final summary of 20 words.

STRATEGY 85

Three-Card Write

Students remember what they write better than they remember what you write. Help them to make stronger connections with Three-Card Write.

Before students begin reading, distribute three index cards to each person. Explain that each student should write "What?" on the first card, "So What?" on the second card, and "Now What?" on the third. Then explain the meaning of each prompt.

"What?" means "What is the most important thing you have read so far?"

"So What?" means "Why is this topic important to you?"

"Now What?" means "What else do you want to know about this topic?"

After students have read a chunk of text, ask each student to pull one of his question cards and take one minute to write a response to it.

Have students share and discuss their responses as a way to build knowledge of the text and glean ideas from other readers.

ANOTHER WAY

English language learners may benefit from drawing their responses rather than writing them. Allow these students to make simple sketches to communicate their responses and inform their discussion of the text.

STRATEGY 86

Calculations in a Zip

When working with students who need a kinesthetic approach to working with number lines, consider creating a number line on an ordinary zipper. Write the numbers 0–10 in permanent marker on the zipper. Students can then manipulate the zipper to count on and to compute simple addition and subtraction problems. For example, to add 3 + 2, a student places the fastener on the number 3, counts up two numbers, and moves the fastener to the number 5.

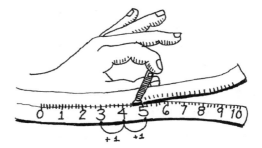

A zipper works well for learning about negative and positive numbers, too. Begin by marking a zero in black marker at the middle of the zipper. To the right of the zero, write the whole numbers 1, 2, 3, 4, and 5. To the left of the zero, use a red marker to write the negative numbers –1, –2, –3, –4, and –5. For example, to add –2 + 4, students place the fastener on –2, count up four numbers, and move the fastener to the positive 2. Rather than memorizing a rule, students can readily see the relationships among the numbers.

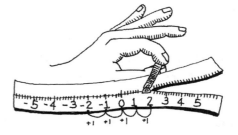

ANOTHER WAY

Use zippers to help young students understand the concept of elapsed time. Mark zippers in increments of hours, half hours, and even quarter hours; have students move the fasteners during timed activities.

One Strip at a Time

Cut math papers into strips. Encourage your discouraged learners to do one strip at a time. Correct each strip as it is completed. This will limit the number of possible mistakes a student can make per paper.

Try cutting the strips vertically as a way to vary the level of difficulty.

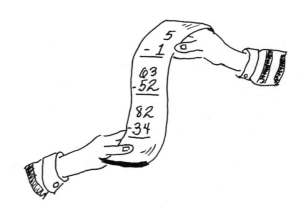

STRATEGY **88**

Go to the Mat for Learning

Mat work is ideal for practicing and achieving success with math facts. This is also a worthwhile activity for students to work on during transitions from one subject/activity to another.

Provide students with a variety of reusable plastic place mats and water-soluble markers. Ask them to practice writing their math facts on the mats.

This practice activity is fun, and students can return to it whenever they have a few free moments.

Post a sign in your classroom that says "Practice Makes Permanent."

Materials

Mats are available in most education stores.

ANOTHER WAY

Have student volunteers design math mats for your resource center. Before publishing the mats, have other students check the facts and operations to make sure everything is accurate. Encourage struggling students to review the math mats with learning partners before quizzes and tests.

STRATEGY 89

Teach with Edibles

Teaching math concepts with edibles is a motivational technique that is not only exciting but delicious, too. This technique rewards students by allowing them to "eat the answers." Students should be taught appropriate precautions to take before handling food.

Favorite edibles include jelly beans, plain M&Ms, Cheerios, Wheat Chex, and Skittles. A 12-segment Hershey chocolate bar is a tasty tool for teaching fractions.

Caution: Always read labels carefully to avoid products that contain peanuts. As you know, these can be harmful or even fatal to some students.

To prepare for food-allergy emergencies, see the reproducible for a Food Allergy Action Plan on pages 137–138 in the Appendix. Be sure to keep a completed copy on hand for any student with serious allergies.

STRATEGY 90

Skill Levels Students Can Deal With

This is not an activity, but rather a great way to presort playing cards to match the skills of a wide range of learners in your classroom. Then, when students play math games, you can put appropriate "skill-level ceilings" on the materials for their practice.

To begin, remove the face cards from several decks of playing cards.

Divide the rest of the cards into piles of aces (to be used for 1s), 2s, 3s, 4s, and so on, through 10s.

Create pre-leveled addition decks that make the following:

- sums through 6 (use cards: ace, 2, and 3)
- sums through 8 (use cards: ace, 2, 3, and 4)

And so on, up to:

- sums through 20 (use cards: ace, 2, 3, 4, 5, 6, 7, 8, 9, and 10)

In each case, make sure that no potential pair of addends exceeds the target sum.

You can also create pre-leveled decks that allow students to practice their multiplication facts.

Note: Casinos use cards once, punch a hole in them, and then discard them. Send a letter written on your school stationery to a casino to request these once-used cards for your classroom.

STRATEGY **91**

Get the Picture

A digital camera can be a powerful tool for differentiating instruction.

One way to use it is to assign students to examine their environment and take photos of concrete examples of a concept they've been studying—perhaps classroom objects that represent different geometric shapes. Use the results for either formative or summative assessment.

You can also use photos—this time images you've captured yourself or downloaded from a website—to access prior knowledge about real-world application of concepts such as lines, angles, or time. As you show the pictures, encourage small groups to discuss what they already know about the topic and to make lists of what they'd like to know about it.

Digital images are an ideal resource for reaching visual learners.

MATH

K–8

Sources for Digital Images

Flickr: flickr.com

Pics4Learning: pics4learning.com

Tools for Slideshows

Smilebox: smilebox.com

Photo Peach: photopeach.com

STRATEGY 92

Number Relationships

Math students at all levels enjoy structured learning competitions that deepen understanding and build fluency. To implement this math game, assign students to small groups or teams. Have one student write a whole number between 1 and 100 on chart paper or a flip chart. Then give team members two minutes to suggest as many equivalents for that number as they can. (See illustration.)

Have the first student in each group record the responses and, when time's up, count the responses. Then have the next student in the group suggest a different number and repeat the process. Continue the game until each team member has taken a turn. The team with the most correct responses wins!

STRATEGY 93

Capture Math Facts with Captive Dice

This is not an activity, but rather a quick and easy way to level and store dice for students to use when practicing their math facts.

Start with small transparent food containers with snap-on lids.

Place a pair of dice or number cubes in each container.

Snap on the lid, and you have captive dice for students to use in practicing their math facts.

Glue those lids so you never lose the dice!

Note: For the multi-ability classroom, use combinations of other polyhedral dice in the containers. Examples include the following:

- octahedron: eight-sided solid (sums to 16; products to 64)

- dodecahedron: twelve-sided solid (sums to 24; products to 144)

- icosahedron: twenty-sided solid (sums to 40; products to 400)

Materials

Dice are available from teacher-supply stores.

STRATEGY 94

I've Got Time

This simple idea helps students tell time to the closest five-minute interval on an analog clock.

Take eleven 3" × 5" index cards. Write a multiple of 5 (from 5 to 55) in bold print on each card. Attach the cards to the wall around the clock as shown in the illustration.

Ask students to tell the time frequently throughout the day.

In her book *Interventions for Struggling Learners*, Gretchen Goodman offers the following helpful idea: Write a student's first name on the hour hand and last name on the minute hand. This helps them remember the order in which to tell time (e.g.: John [hour] Grant [minute] = 1:28.)

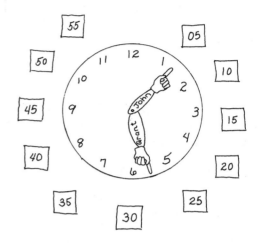

STRATEGY 95

Triangular Number Bonds

Triangular flash cards reinforce number-family relationships for both addition/subtraction and multiplication/division facts.

You can make your own examples to use with a document camera by cutting out triangles from old manila folders and then writing fact families on the triangles. (See the illustration.)

If you have a job center or students who like to be helpers, they can cut out more triangles and write a variety of fact families on them. Place these flash cards in the math center for student use.

Materials

If you prefer not to make your own, you can also buy ready-made triangular flash cards. They are a product of Trend Enterprises Inc. and are available at teacher stores, through teacher-supply catalogs, at some office-supply stores, and online at trendenterprises.com.

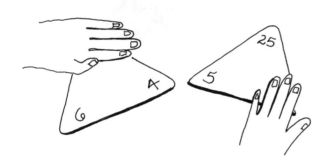

STRATEGY 96

What's My Name?

You will need a name tag for each student in the room.

On each tag, in the space where the student's name would normally be written, write a math expression the class is studying. Do not include the answer on the name tag.

Hand out the name tags, have students wear them, and ask them to mingle throughout the room learning the new names of their classmates. For example, Jim's name tag says "3×7" instead of "Jim." Thus, his new name is "21." For the week, everyone must address Jim as "21."

Students can get new names as often as you deem appropriate: daily, twice a week, or weekly.

This activity gets students involved and motivated to learn math facts in a different way.

STRATEGY 97

Box One, Circle the Other

Avoid the confusion and common mistakes made by students when computing math examples with mixed operations.

On a page of math examples, circle the addition examples and box the subtraction examples.

Have the students do all the addition examples first and correct them. Next, have the students complete all the subtraction examples and correct them.

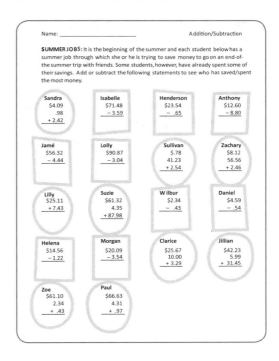

Keep Your Numbers in Line

Prevent careless computation errors made by students with "drifting" handwriting by turning lined paper sideways to facilitate proper number placement. Use graph paper for long division.

Alternatively, make copies of the reproducibles in the Appendix on pages 139–142 and have students use those grids for their calculations.

GOOD LUCK WITH YOUR ADDITION!

```
  3 4 6      6 3 1      4 4 8
+ 5 5 0    + 7 8 0    + 5 5 1


  8 7 0      3 3 6      4 0 0 8
  9 4 0      4 7 7      2 5 7 3
+ 6 8 8    + 2 3 6    + 7 6 0 1
```

Cross Out Every Other Math Example

With a light-colored marker, cross out every other math example on a page. Use this as a way to adjust the assignment and create a reasonable workload for discouraged and/or overwhelmed learners.

The examples that are crossed out become either the student's homework assignment or the next day's math lesson.

This curriculum modification is most beneficial to students who work at a much slower pace than others.

Name: _____   Adding

CLASS TRIP
The students in the class below are soon leaving for a class trip. Who will be bringing the most money on the trip? The least? Solve these problems to find out the answer!

Simone	**Gail**	**Nomar**	**Jackson**
$4.09	$5.23	$7.02	$8.12
.98	71.48	23.54	56.56
+ 6.42	+ 3.59	+ .65	+ 2.46

Roberto	**Sky**	**Gregory**	**Morgan**
$56.32	$90.87	$.78	$.13
4.44	3.04	41.23	.54
+ 23.87	+ .45	+ 2.54	+ 4.59

Lucy	**Sarah**	**Washington**	**Aubrey**
25.11	$61.32	$59.00	$42.23
+ 7.43	4.35	2.34	5.99
	+ 87.98	+ .43	+ 31.45

Hector	**Monica**	**Clara**	
$90.01	$20.09	$25.67	
14.56	3.54	10.00	
+ 1.22	+ 23.42	+ 3.29	

Josephine	**Regis**	**Althea**	
$61.10	$66.63	$.59	
2.34	4.31	12.60	
+ .43	+ .97	+ 8.80	

STRATEGY 100

Calling All Numbers

One way to fit in more meaningful math practice is through quality anchor activities that students can complete when they've finished another assignment and have extra time. Here's one that recycles the pages from an old phone book.

Instruct each student to select a page from a phone directory and use it to complete specific tasks you assign. Depending on students' skill levels, you might choose any of these tasks:

- Highlight five numbers that are even numbers.

- Highlight five numbers that are odd numbers.

- Underline two phone numbers for which the sum of the digits is exactly 25.

- Circle the numbers in a phone number that are multiples of 3.

- Underline the numbers in a phone number that are multiples of 4.

- Create the sum of 60 by adding four single digits to any phone number.

- Create the total of 22 by subtracting four digits from any phone number.

- Draw a box around the median number in any phone number.

- Find the average of the digits in that same phone number.

- Using addition, subtraction, multiplication, and/or division, create equations with the seven digits for which the answer is 25.

- Find 3 seven-digit numbers that are multiples of 2. Repeat to find multiples of 3, 4, 5, 6, 8, 9, and 10.

STRATEGY 101

Numbers in the News

Provide pages from any newspaper for students to use as the basis for anchor activities (work to be undertaken as meaningful practice after other assignments have been completed). On a chart—or in a file folder that students can take to their seats—post questions for student responses. Consider your students' math skills and create your own questions or choose some from the following ideas:

- Find whole numbers and highlight hundreds, tens, and ones in different colors.

- Find and underline metric measurements.

- Circle fractions.

- On a weather map for the country, identify the city with the lowest temperature and the one with the highest temperature. Calculate the difference between the two readings.

- During football season, turn to the sports section and find the score of one game. Create an organized list of the possible ways each score could have been attained. After you complete your list, read the full article about the game to see how each team actually scored its points. For example, if one team scored 21 points, that team could have had 3 touchdowns with extra points, 7 field goals, 3 touchdowns without extra points plus 1 field goal, and so on.

ANOTHER WAY

Invite older students to follow specific stocks and chart their closing values over one week's time. Then have them calculate the difference in share prices, if any, in dollars and cents. Challenge students to determine the percentage of change in value.

STRATEGY 102

Focusing on the Facts

Multiplication charts can be too "busy" for many learners, but students can slide multiplication and division facts into focus by using color strips. The highlighting strips reinforce fact-family relationships.

You will need acetate in two different colors. You will also need copies of the reproducible for a multiplication chart on page 143 in the Appendix—one copy for each student.

Cut two strips of acetate, one in each color, for each student. The strips should be the same width as the rows and columns of the chart.

Place one colored strip on a column of the chart and place a different-colored strip over a row. For example, try placing one strip, vertically, on the 4s column. Place the other colored strip horizontally on the 3s row. You will see the product, 12, come into focus.

Show students how to slide the strips to bring multiplication and division facts into focus.

Materials

Colored transparency sheets are sold in office-supply stores. A less expensive option is to use colored, transparent book report covers, also available at most office-supply stores.

1	2	3	4	5	6	7	8	9	10	11	12
2	4	6	8	10	12	14	16	18	20	22	24
3	6	9	12	15	18	21	24	27	30	33	36
4	8	12	16	20	24	28	32	36	40	44	48
5	10	15	20	25	30	35	40	45	50	55	60
6	12	18	24	30	36	42	48	54	60	66	72
7	14	21	28	35	42	49	56	63	70	77	84
8	16	24	32	40	48	56	64	72	80	88	96
9	18	27	36	45	54	63	72	81	90	99	108
10	20	30	40	50	60	70	80	90	100	110	120
11	22	33	44	55	66	77	88	99	110	121	132
12	24	36	48	60	72	84	96	108	120	132	144

ANOTHER WAY

Fortify math connections for English language learners with real-world problem solving. For example, each center row in an auditorium accommodates 10 students and 1 teacher. There are 11 rows. How many students can sit in the center rows? How many teachers? Have students use graph paper to find the correct answers.

STRATEGY 103

Equivalent Fractions Before Your Eyes

A multiplication chart is a great tool for showing number patterns and relationships, and it's ideal for students to use for finding equivalent fractions.

Start with the reproducible on page 143 in the Appendix and some colored acetate strips.

Place one acetate strip horizontally on the first row of numbers on the multiplication chart. Next, place the second strip directly below it.

As you look at the two rows covered by the colored strips, think "fractions" instead of two rows of numbers. You should see the equivalent fractions for 1/2: 2/4, 4/8, 6/12, and so on.

Next, place the strips across the rows beginning with 2 and 3. Now the equivalent fractions for 2/3 become clear.

As you move the colored strips down the rows, equivalent fractions through 11/12 are shown on the chart.

Students can also place the colored strips on nonadjacent rows to find the equivalent fractions for examples such as 3/8, 2/7, 5/9, 6/10, and so on.

1	2	3	4	5	6	7	8	9	10	11	12
2	4	6	8	10	12	14	16	18	20	22	24
3	6	9	12	15	18	21	24	27	30	33	36
4	8	12	16	20	24	28	32	36	40	44	48
5	10	15	20	25	30	35	40	45	50	55	60
6	12	18	24	30	36	42	48	54	60	66	72
7	14	21	28	35	42	49	56	63	70	77	84
8	16	24	32	40	48	56	64	72	80	88	96
9	18	27	36	45	54	63	72	81	90	99	108
10	20	30	40	50	60	70	80	90	100	110	120
11	22	33	44	55	66	77	88	99	110	121	132
12	24	36	48	60	72	84	96	108	120	132	144

STRATEGY 104

Howdy, Partner Factor!

This method teaches students how to factor numbers in a way that reinforces multiplication/division relationships.

Refer to the illustration for a visual cue on this method.

To begin, each student draws a vertical line on her paper.

She then writes the "target number" (i.e., the number she is factoring) in the upper right corner, to the right of the line.

Next, she writes the number 1 opposite the target number, to the left of the vertical line. (The number 1 is a factor of every number.)

Now the questioning begins: "Is 2 a factor?" If 2 is a factor of the number, each student writes a 2 below the 1, to the left of the vertical line. Then she puts its "partner" directly opposite it, to the right of the vertical line.

Students continue with 3, 4, 5, and so on, until they have listed all the factors of the target number.

Not Your Average Math Practice

This is a great strategy for finding the arithmetic mean or average of a set of numbers and helping students understand that when finding the average, they are trying to equalize unequal values.

Begin by giving each student a copy of the Hundreds Chart on page 130. Students will also need transparent counters (bingo chips work well) and a calculator to check their computations.

Tell students to find the blocks for the numbers 1, 3, 21, and 23, as shown in the illustration, and to place counters of the same color on each of these blocks. Then have students calculate the sum of these four numbers (48).

Next, ask students to divide the sum by the number of blocks they added together (4) and to cover the block that matches the answer (12). Have students describe the pattern they see. Then ask them to choose four new numbers and predict the average.

This activity also works using calendars and multiplication charts. The key is to find a square or rectangle on the chart with an odd number of blocks on each side. The average number is always the center number (central value) in the group of blocks.

Hundreds Chart

ANOTHER WAY

To help learners visualize and manipulate number patterns, start with a piece of cardboard and affix a transparency on which you've drawn an extra-large grid with indelible marker. Switch to a dry-erase marker and create a number pattern in the first blocks of the grid. Hand over the grid and ask the student to continue the pattern.

STRATEGY 106

What's Your Response?

The use of response cards is a management technique that helps you assess the understanding of individual students within a large-group setting.

Give each student three white index cards.

Each student writes "YES" on the first card, "NO" on the second, and a question mark on the third.

Students can store their response cards in library-book pockets kept inside their desks or binders.

Instruct students that no one is allowed to look at anyone else's response card, nor is anyone to ask another student how he responded. When asked a question, each student should choose the appropriate response card and then hold it up just below his chin for the teacher to check his understanding.

Tell students you will ask them to take out their response cards periodically throughout the day to respond to instructions or directions. For example, you might read aloud and stop to ask the class to predict whether they think a particular event will happen in the story. In math class, you might write a number on the board and ask the class to respond about whether they agree that it is an even number. You might also give multi-step directions before a lesson and ask the students to use their response cards to show whether they understand.

This technique helps students learn to focus and pay attention.

STRATEGY 107

Anecdotal Records

Patterns of information help teachers make decisions about interventions that work with students. Anecdotal records are an effective way to keep track of your observations during "kid-watching" time.

Photocopy the Monthly Manager (see reproducible in the Appendix on page 144) for each student in your class.

When you want to record an observation about a student, take out that student's monthly manager and write the following:

- Next to B, write the behavior you are watching.

- Next to I, write the intervention you are trying.

- Next to R, write the result of the intervention.

This type of record shows patterns of behaviors, what interventions you have already used in an effort to help, and the result of the efforts. This information is helpful for making instructional decisions for students.

The Monthly Manager

Month of _September_   Student's Name _Robin Jenkins_

	Monday	Tuesday	Wednesday	Thursday	Friday
Week of 9/23 to 9/27	B: Writes "My brother don't" in his narrative. I: Demonstrated how to whisper read into the Phonics Phone to catch usage concern. R: Corrected 3 out of 9 usage concerns.	B: I: R:	B: I: R:	B: I: R:	B: I: R:
Week of ___ to ___	B: I: R:	B: I: R:	B: I: R:	B: I: R:	B: I: R:
Week of ___ to ___	B: I: R:	B: I: R:	B: I: R:	B: I: R:	B: I: R:
Week of ___ to ___	B: I: R:	B: I: R:	B: I: R:	B: I: R:	B: I: R:
Week of ___ to ___	B: I: R:	B: I: R:	B: I: R:	B: I: R:	B: I: R:

B = Behavior   I = Intervention   R = Result

Poll the Audience

Hand-held wireless response devices—"clickers"—are innovative assessment accessories for the classroom. During a lesson, you pose questions either verbally or on PowerPoint slides, and students use the devices to click on their responses. The software that comes with the clickers records the results; you can view the data privately on the computer screen or project percentage responses for the class to see. The advantage, of course, is that you can check for comprehension and modify instruction in real time.

You can also collect response data from pre- and post assessments. Use this data to identify areas of weakness and create small groups based on skill level or develop mini-lessons for the future.

Student Response Systems

eInstruction: einstruction.com/products/student-response-systems

Mouse Mischief: microsoft.com/multipoint/mouse-mischief/en-us/default.aspx

ActivExpression by Promethean: prometheanworld.com/server.php?show=nav.19269

SMART Response Systems: smarttech.com/us/Solutions/Education+Solutions/Products+for+education/Complementary+hardware+products/SMART+Response

ANOTHER WAY

Use student response systems to streamline your quizzes or tests, too. After students answer quiz or test questions with the clickers, the system automatically calculates grades, saving you valuable time. Instead of getting bogged down in grading, you can focus on using the scores to drive your instruction.

STRATEGY 109

Level the Playing Field

Separate language from computation by using a copier to eliminate word problems from math papers with basic math examples.

Non-readers and English language learners will be able to experience math-computation success with this simple curriculum modification.

Word problems can be presented in due time when the student becomes a better reader and/or English proficient.

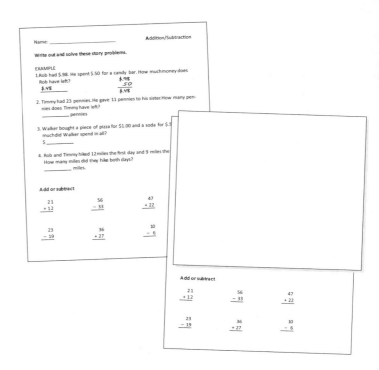

Understanding instructions is essential to proceeding correctly. Help struggling students find and understand key words in written instructions. For example, the first command in the illustration—*Write out and solve*—requires two operations; the second command—*Add or subtract*—requires only one.

STRATEGY 110

One, Two, Three... Go!

This process helps teachers ensure a student is correctly completing a math process or writing spelling words before doing several examples on her own. Practice makes permanent, so you want to be sure that what the student is practicing is correct.

When learning new algorithms in math or writing new spelling words, some students get off to an incorrect start and reinforce it by completing several examples, if not an entire page, before a teacher catches the problem.

To prevent this, use the One, Two, Three...Go! method of monitoring student work. A student does one example and then checks with you or a pre-assigned student. If the completed example is correct, the student then does two examples in a row and returns for feedback. If those examples are done accurately, the student completes three in a row and checks in.

If those are correct, tell the student it's a go! He can complete the assignment, reinforcing the concept that practice makes permanent.

STRATEGY 111

Personal-Learning Time Lines

This is a unique strategy for journaling. Use rolls of adding-machine tape that students can unroll at the end of each day to capture the day's important learning.

Each student needs his own personal roll of paper. You can store them all together in one safe box, or students can keep them in their desks or cubbies.

During the last 20 minutes of the school day, have a reflect-and-regroup time. Each student takes out her learning time line and unrolls it to the next free space. Here she writes the date on the space and then records or draws important highlights of the day's learning.

Students can write examples of math problems they worked on, new vocabulary words learned, titles of completed books, illustrations of special events, poems they have written, and so forth.

The time lines help students see their own learning in progress, and they also serve as excellent records for parents to keep at the end of the school year.

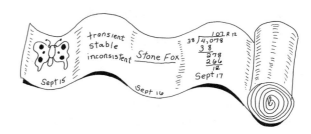

ANOTHER WAY

At the beginning of the school year, invite all students to set individual learning goals. Set aside time for them to track their progress toward reaching their goals. Encourage each student to keep a personal journal, a great tool for recording progress, evaluating setbacks, and celebrating success in all content areas.

STRATEGY 112

High-Tech Assessment

At the beginning of the school year, start a personal video for each student, as well as one for the entire class. This is an excellent way to capture the learning and the memories. Video recording also provides immediate visual and auditory feedback for students to use in assessing and improving their learning.

Throughout the year, record individual successes and important group events on the video.

Weave in requirements for your state or Common Core standards as students give video presentations.

Allow some students to submit video recordings as projects to show what they have learned.

STRATEGY 113

Student-Led Conferences

A student-led conference involves the student, parent(s), and teacher(s). It creates a critical partnership with the parent(s) or guardian(s) and draws them into their child's education beyond the typical "bake sale" involvement.

Entire professional books on the topic of student-led conferences are available, but the basic principle is that this is a conference that both the student and parent(s) attend.

During the conference, the student reviews and explains her portfolio or work samples from the marking period. You discuss the grading system, and together you, the student, and the parent(s) establish goals to help with study or academic skills. At the next conference, the first order of business is to review progress toward these goals.

STRATEGY 114

Here's Looking at You, Kid

Report cards should demonstrate a student's growth in all areas of instruction for the marking period. The problem with many graded report cards is the difficulty of attaching a letter grade to student performance. Anecdotal reports can be time consuming, and sometimes parents do not take the time to read them.

An alternative kind of report card (see reproducible on page 145 in the Appendix) is a one-page summary of the marking period's focus of instruction and a record of the student's progress. It is a straightforward form.

This report card is also responsive to the needs of special-education students who have modified curriculums and for whom a traditional report card is not appropriate.

(see reproducible on page 145 in the Appendix)

ANOTHER WAY

Maintaining an open dialogue about assessment is important for building trust and respect between teacher and student. Reinforce your commitment by sharing your observations and evaluations on each student's progress on a regular basis. Invite your students to respond in writing. Use their comments as jumping-off points for discussion and clarification.

STRATEGY **115**

Facts in a Flash

This game is a great activity for reviewing, practicing, and assessing students' learning of a particular skill or unit of study.

You will need one index card for each student in your class.

To begin, create a T chart on a sheet of paper. At the top of the left column, write the phrase "I Have," and at the top of the right column, write the phrase "Who Has?"

Choose a skill or unit of study for review. For example, to review math facts, you might create a T chart like this:

I Have	Who Has?
25	The square root of my number?
5	This number, plus 14 more?
19	This number, take away 7?
12	This number doubled?
24	This number, plus 6, minus 5?
25	

The number or fact that is your beginning point should also be your end point.

On each card, write sentences based on one entire row from your T chart. For example, one card might read, "I have 25. Who has the square root of my number?"

When playing this game, the class sits in a circle. One student starts the fast-fact session. When his answer comes up again, the game is over.

Try beating a timer!

STRATEGY **116**

Realistic Rubrics

Rubrics function as diagnostic, prescriptive, and evaluative tools. They help us assess individual, as well as small and large group instructional needs. Rubrics allow us to focus on interventions, methods, or strategies that are appropriate for students. They also provide the criteria through which student performance will be evaluated for specific projects, assignments, or units of study.

You can create your own rubrics for most aspects of your classroom program. Just follow three simple steps.

First, decide on the purpose of your rubric. For example, you might want to assess, plan, and/or monitor the progress of your students' math fact fluency.

Next, determine the mastery levels and use these as labels for each column on your grid.

Finally, add indicators below each mastery label that describe representative performance levels.

Fluent Facts!	**Accurate, Not Fluent**	**Emergent Learning Stage**
30 facts/min. paper & pencil	15 facts/min. paper & pencil	>10 facts/min. paper & pencil
40 facts/min. oral	20 facts/min. oral	>15 facts/min. oral
Knows facts at a level of automaticity.	Automatic knowledge of math facts in instructional situations is inconsistent.	Needs intervention or assistance most of the time.

STRATEGY 117
Survey Says

Before teaching new material, use surveys to assess students' background knowledge. Free online survey makers offer easy-to-use tools for creating pre-assessments.

Simply register online with one of the sites, and then design your own survey, writing multiple-choice or true-false questions. Before administering the assessment, be sure to explain to students that the goal is to find out what they already know and that their answers will not be graded. Use individual and collective data from completed surveys to inform and modify your instruction.

Online Sources for Creating Surveys

Quiz Snack: quizsnack.com

Survey Monkey: surveymonkey.com

Zoomerang: zoomerang.com

ANOTHER WAY

After collecting the survey data, you may find that the students have a solid understanding of the content already. Instead of starting with the basics, go ahead and provide instruction on the next level. The opposite is also true. If you find students have a very limited understanding or none at all, start at square one.

STRATEGY 118

Dueling Charts

Select a topic that your students have been studying, such as the Civil War.

Write the topic phrase (in this case, "Civil War") horizontally across the top of each of two charts.

Divide students into two teams.

Each team lines up in front of one chart.

On a given signal, a student from each team goes to the chart and writes vertically a phrase pertaining to something studied in the unit. The phrase must start with the first letter of the phrase you have written on the chart. For example, "Civil War began in 1861." The next student from each team writes a phrase that starts with the second letter of the phrase you have written on the chart, and so on.

The first team to finish gets a high-five from the other team.

STRATEGY 119
Post What You Know

Checking for understanding is an ongoing process in the differentiated classroom. Exit slips—short, written student responses to a prompt given at the end of a class or task—work well as an informal assessment strategy. Traditionally, students have written their responses on paper or index cards. Now, you can boost engagement by having students respond online with digital "sticky notes."

Simply create an online bulletin board on a site such as Corkboard or Wall Wisher. Students type their responses on the "sticky notes" and post them on the question board; be sure to have each learner include his name or class number, so you can identify individual responses. You can easily review the responses and adjust your next lesson accordingly.

Online Bulletin Boards

Corkboard: corkboard.me/simple

Wall Wisher: wallwisher.com

ANOTHER WAY

To tier your assessment, you can provide multiple prompts, based on the skill levels of different groups of students. It's easy to create a different wall or board for each prompt, and then you can simply give each student a link to the appropriate location for responding to his assigned question.

Appendix

Page	Reproducible	Strategy	Page
122	Student Problem Report	No Problem!	1
123	Left-Hander Factoids	"Lefties" Have Different Needs	6
124	10 Homework Tips for Parents	Plotting Homework	7
125	Intervention Plan	It's a Plan	11
126	"I Can" Slips	No Can'ts Allowed	15
127	Clock Partners	Clock Partners	26
128	Multiple Intelligence Scavenger Hunt	We're Going on a Scavenger Hunt!	29
129	Buzz Sheet	The Classroom Buzz	32
130	Hundreds Chart	You Can Count on Bingo Chips	38
		Not Your Average Math Practice	105
131	Focus Frame	Using a Focus Frame to Get the Picture	46
132	Sliding Mask	Sliding Mask	47
133	Self-Test for Scotopic Sensitivity Syndrome	Bring It into Focus	59
134	4-6-8	4-6-8	68
135	Word Map	Word Map	70
136	C.P.S.R. Starters	C.P.S.R. (Copy-Pair-Share-Respond)	74
137–138	Food Allergy Action Plan	Teach with Edibles	89
139	Good Luck with Your Addition!	Keep Your Numbers in Line	98
140	Good Luck with Your Subtraction!	Keep Your Numbers in Line	98
141	Good Luck with Your Multiplication!	Keep Your Numbers in Line	98
142	Good Luck with Your Division!	Keep Your Numbers in Line	98
143	Multiplication Chart	Focusing on the Facts	102
		Equivalent Fractions Before Your Eyes	103
144	The Monthly Manager	Anecdotal Records	107
145	Report Card	Here's Looking at You, Kid	114

Student Problem Report

Filed by: _____

Date: _____

Description of problem: _____

_____

_____

Location of problem: _____

_____

Persons involved: _____

_____

Witnesses: _____

What did the witnesses do? _____

_____

How do you feel about what happened? _____

_____

How do you think the other student feels? _____

_____

List two things you might have done to solve the problem or prevent it from happening:

1. _____

2. _____

What do you think the teacher should do about this problem?

_____

_____

Student signature: _____

Left-Hander Factoids

- There are twice as many left-handed boys as girls.

- Left-handers are twice as likely to qualify for membership in Mensa, the high-IQ society.

- Left-handed people tend to have more industrial accidents.

- Left-handed people have a more acute sense of humor. Left-handed comics include W.C. Fields, Harpo Marx, Carol Burnett, David Letterman, Charlie Chaplin, Richard Pryor, Jay Leno, and Dick Van Dyke.

- The French horn is valved for the left hand.

- Michelangelo was left-handed.

- Toll booths favor left-handers.

- Ben Franklin was left-handed.

- Hand preference is evident by age five.

- Joan of Arc was left-handed.

Adapted from: *Left-Handed Kids: Why Are They So Different?* and *The Natural Superiority of the Left-Hander* by James T. DeKay, and *Left-Handed in a Right-Handed World* by Jeff Goldsmith.

10 Homework Tips for Parents

1. Set aside a specific time for your child to do homework each night. This will help eliminate procrastination.

2. Designate a quiet and well-lit place for your child to work.

3. Protect your child from annoying distractions. Establish a quiet zone.

4. Be sure your child has the necessary materials and supplies at hand to support his homework (e.g., pencil, pen, eraser, pencil sharpener, ruler, paper, etc.). Create a "school-office" atmosphere for your child.

5. Stay in close proximity to your child during homework time.

6. Have your child invite a study buddy over so they can do homework together.

7. If you are unable to help your child with an assignment, find a relative, neighbor, or older student who is willing to help out.

8. Always check your child's homework for quality and completeness.

9. Connect with your child's school on a regular basis. Know the school's homework policy, ask how you can support what the school is doing, and ask about the amount of homework and the purpose of the assignments. Inquire if daily and long-term homework assignments are posted on the school's website.

10. Monitor any time your child spends on the computer.

Intervention Plan

Interventionist/Teacher: _____

Target Area _____ Initial Status _____

Tier _____ Intervention _____ Goal _____

Progress Monitoring Data

DATE	Freq/Duration of Intervention	Results	Anecdotal Observations

Interventionist/Teacher: _____

Target Area _____ Initial Status _____

Tier _____ Intervention _____ Goal _____

Progress Monitoring Data

DATE	Freq/Duration of Intervention	Results	Anecdotal Observations

Interventionist/Teacher: _____

Target Area _____ Initial Status _____

Tier _____ Intervention _____ Goal _____

Progress Monitoring Data

DATE	Freq/Duration of Intervention	Results	Anecdotal Observations

Adapted from *Intervention Documentation Folder*

© 2008 Gretchen Goodman

"I Can" Slips

I can

_____

_____

_____

_____

Name

_____

Date

_____

I can

_____

_____

_____

_____

Name

_____

Date

_____

I can

_____

_____

_____

_____

Name

_____

Date

_____

I can

_____

_____

_____

_____

Name

_____

Date

_____

Clock Partners

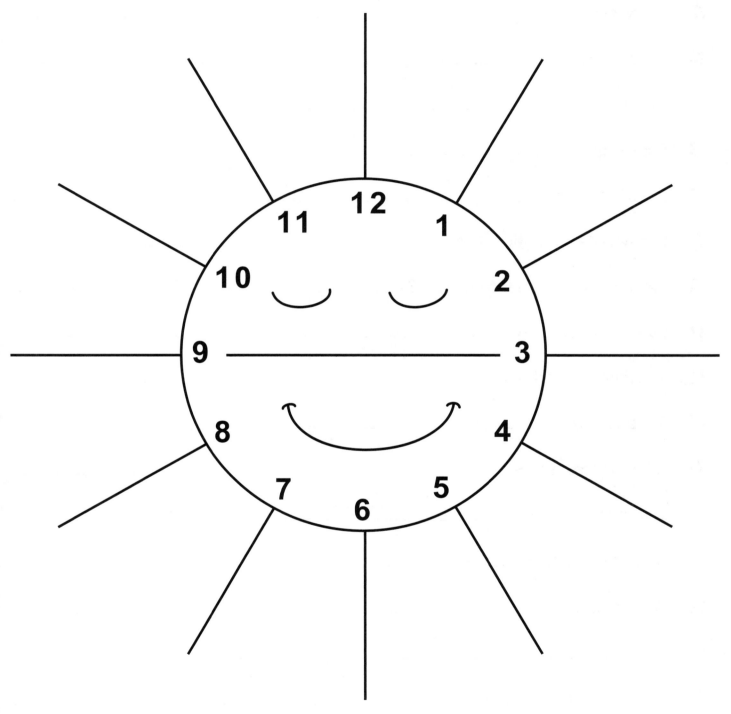

Multiple Intelligence Scavenger Hunt

Find someone who:

- ◼ Reads every night _____
- ◼ Keeps a journal _____
- ◼ Makes quilts _____
- ◼ Fixes engines _____
- ◼ Sings in a chorus _____
- ◼ Can whistle our national anthem _____
- ◼ Can finish this sequence: 1, 1, 2, 3, 5, 8 . . . _____
- ◼ Can define icosahedron _____
- ◼ Will recite a short poem _____
- ◼ Plays a sport _____
- ◼ Takes dance lessons _____
- ◼ Plays an instrument _____
- ◼ Loves to entertain _____
- ◼ Can juggle _____
- ◼ Makes art _____
- ◼ Enjoys hiking or camping _____
- ◼ Likes to take things apart _____

BUZZ SHEET

DISCUSS THE QUESTIONS WITH YOUR PARTNER

GETTING STARTED

1. WHAT IS YOUR FAVORITE . . . WHY?

* PLACE TO GO ON VACATION
* WAY TO TRAVEL
* PLACE TO EAT
* PLACE TO SPEND THE NIGHT

FEELING COMFORTABLE

2. WHEN WAS THE LAST TIME YOU FELT ONE OF THESE . . . WHY?

* HAPPY   * PUT DOWN
* COOL   * EMBARRASSED
* ZANY   * EXCITED

CURRENT FEELINGS

3. WHICH THREE MENU ITEMS BEST DESCRIBE YOUR FEELINGS NOW? WHY?

* HAMBURGER   * MILKSHAKE
* CHERRY COKE   * PIZZA
* OREO COOKIES   * JELLO

Hundreds Chart

1	2	3	4	5	6	7	8	9	10
11	12	13	14	15	16	17	18	19	20
21	22	23	24	25	26	27	28	29	30
31	32	33	34	35	36	37	38	39	40
41	42	43	44	45	46	47	48	49	50
51	52	53	54	55	56	57	58	59	60
61	62	63	64	65	66	67	68	69	70
71	72	73	74	75	76	77	78	79	80
81	82	83	84	85	86	87	88	89	90
91	92	93	94	95	96	97	98	99	100

Focus Frame

Directions

Cut out and trace Focus Frame pattern below onto poster board or equivalent stock paper. Cut out focus frame from poster board, then cut along lines (indicated on pattern) on frame section A. Insert frame section B into section A to form a movable box. Slide the Focus Frame to adjust for the amount of space needed.

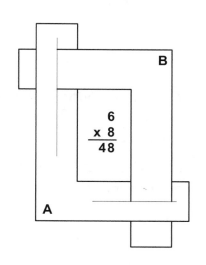

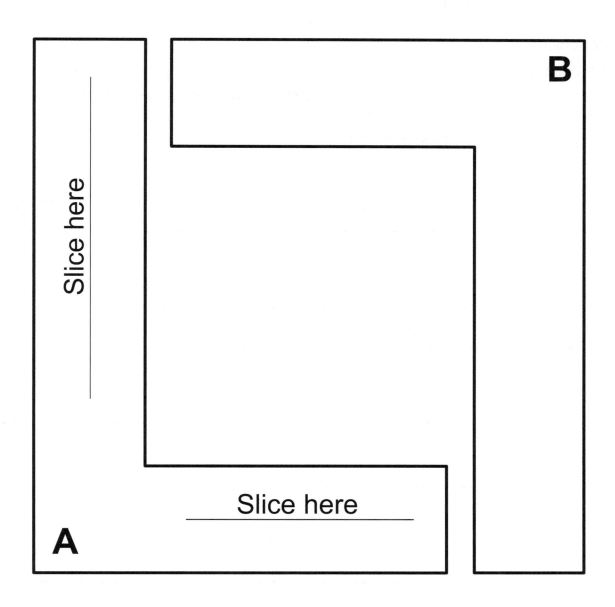

Sliding Mask

Directions

- Cut out mask (A) and strip (B) pattern and trace onto poster board or equivalent stock paper.

- Cut along lines for inside box in mask and remove paper to reveal open window.

- Cut slices as marked in mask.

- Place open window over desired text/ problems. Insert strip as shown in illustration, and slide strip from underneath the mask to cover or reveal selected text/problems.

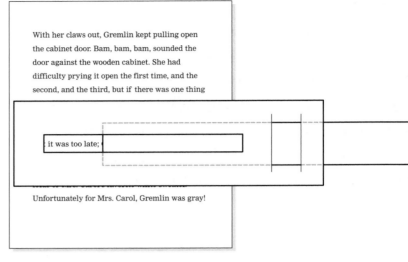

Note: The Sliding Mask can be modified by taping a colored plastic strip (colored acetate or frosted colored overlays, for example) over the window opening. This is particularly helpful for students who experience difficulty when reading black print on white paper. See page 59 for more information on colored overlays.

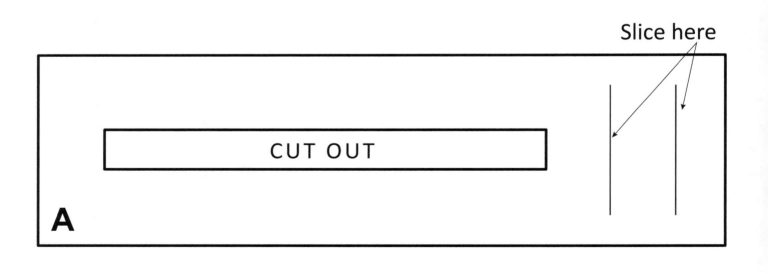

Self-Test for Scotopic Sensitivity Syndrome

Do you or someone you know have difficulty reading?
Take the following test:

	YES	NO
Do you skip words or lines when reading?		
Do you reread lines?		
Do you lose your place?		
Are you easily distracted when reading?		
Do you need to take breaks often?		
Do you find it harder to read the longer you read?		
Do you get headaches when you read?		
Do your eyes get red and watery?		
Does reading make you tired?		
Do you blink or squint?		
Do you prefer to read in dim light?		
Do you read close to the page?		
Do you use your finger or other markers?		
Do you get restless, active, or fidgety when reading?		

If you answered yes to three or more of these questions,
then you might be experiencing the effects of a perception
problem called Scotopic Sensitivity Syndrome.

Adapted with permission from Reading by the Colors by Helen L. Irlen, Penguin Putnam/Perigee Div. Publishers.

4-6-8

Characters	Settings	Events
1.	1.	1.
	2.	2.
2.	3.	3.
	4.	4.
3.	5.	5.
	6.	6.
4.		7.
		8.

WORD MAP

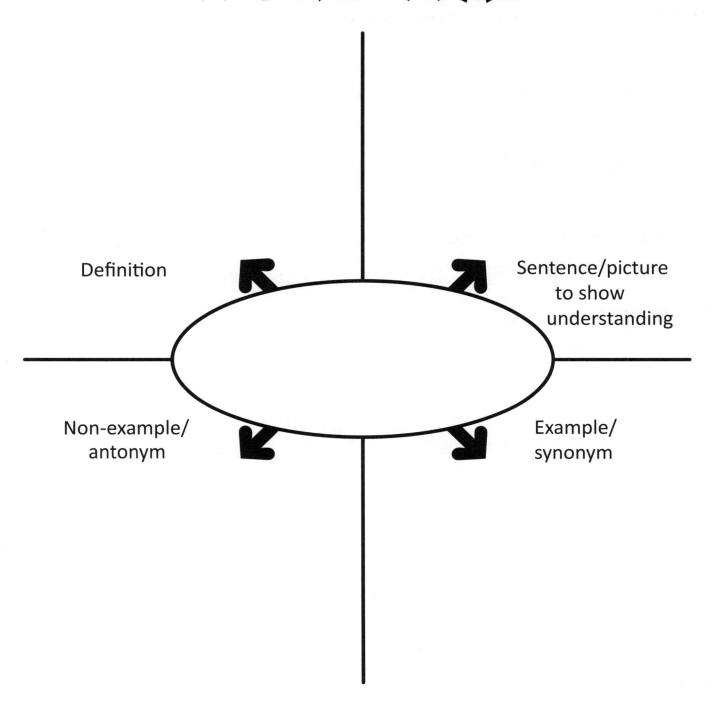

Definition

Sentence/picture to show understanding

Non-example/ antonym

Example/ synonym

C.P.S.R. Starters

What did you think about the sentences your partner picked?

- I liked this part because _____

- I didn't like this part because _____

- This scene made me think about _____

- I wonder _____

- I didn't understand why _____

- I can't believe _____

- I think _____

- I feel _____

- I wish _____ had happened.

- If I were _____ (character's name), I _____

_____ .

Food Allergy Action Plan

Place Child's Picture Here

Allergy to: _____

Student's Name: _____ D.O.B.: _____ Teacher: _____

Asthmatic: ☐ Yes, high risk for severe reaction ☐ No

SIGNS OF AN ALLERGIC REACTION

Systems | Symptoms

- Mouth — itching and swelling of the lips, tongue, or mouth
- Throat* — itching and/or a sense of tightness in the throat, hoarseness, and hacking cough
- Skin — hives, itchy rash, and/or swelling about the face or extremities
- Gut — nausea, abdominal cramps, vomiting, and/or diarrhea
- Lung* — shortness of breath, repetitive coughing, and/or wheezing
- Heart* — "thready" pulse, "passing out"

The severity of symptoms can quickly change.

* These specific symptoms can potentially progress to a life-threatening situation.

ACTION FOR MINOR REACTION

1. If only symptom(s) are: _____, give _____
(medication/dose/route)

_____

Then call:

2. Mother: _____, Father: _____, or emergency contacts.

3. Dr. _____ at _____.

If condition does not improve within 10 minutes, follow steps for Major Reaction, below.

ACTION FOR MAJOR REACTION

1. If ingestion is suspected and/or symptom(s) are: _____

give _____ IMMEDIATELY!
(medication/dose/route)

Then call:

2. Rescue Squad (ask for advanced life support)

3. Mother: _____, Father: _____, or emergency contacts.

4. Dr. _____ at _____.

DO NOT HESITATE TO CALL RESCUE SQUAD!

Parent's
Signature: _____ Date: _____

Doctor's
Signature: _____ Date: _____

Food Allergy Action Plan, *continued*

EMERGENCY CONTACTS	TRAINED STAFF MEMBERS
1. _____ Relation: _____ Phone: _____	**1.** _____ Room: _____
2. _____ Relation: _____ Phone: _____	**2.** _____ Room: _____
3. _____ Relation: _____ Phone: _____	**3.** _____ Room: _____

EpiPen ® and EpiPen ® Jr. Directions

1. Pull off gray safety cap.

2. Place black tip on outer thigh (always apply to thigh).

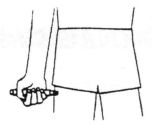

3. Using a quick motion, press hard into thigh until Auto-Injector or mechanism functions. Hold in place and count to 10. The EpiPen ® unit should then be removed and discarded. Massage the injection area for 10 seconds.

For children with multiple food allergies, use one form for each food.

To learn more about the Food Allergy and Anaphylaxis Network, go to: foodallergy.org.
Adapted with permission from The Food Allergy and Anaphylaxis Network.

The Food Allergy & Anaphylaxis Network

Good Luck with Your Addition!

Good Luck with Your Subtraction!

Good Luck with Your Multiplication!

Good Luck with Your Division!

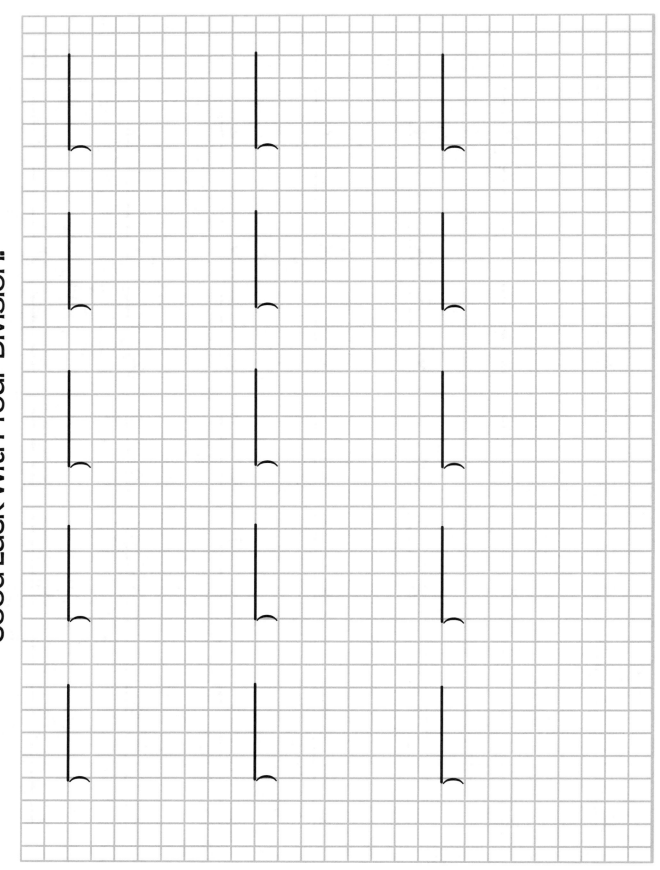

Does McDonald's Sell Cheeseburgers Rare?

Divide ÷   Multiply ×   Subtract −   Check ✓   Bring down   Remainder

Multiplication Chart

Directions for Focusing on the Facts

1. Locate two sheets of colored acetate.

2. Cut out two different colored strips (1/2" × 6").

3. Choose a "fact family," such as 4 × 7 = 28, on the chart. Lay one colored strip along the 4s row. Lay the other down on the 7s column.

4. The product (or dividend) appears at the intersection of the two strips.

Directions for Equivalent Fractions Before Your Eyes

1. Locate two sheets of colored acetate.

2. Cut out two different colored strips (1/2" × 6").

3. Find equivalent fractions by placing one strip across one row of numbers and a second strip across another row of numbers.

1	2	3	4	5	6	7	8	9	10	11	12
2	4	6	8	10	12	14	16	18	20	22	24
3	6	9	12	15	18	21	24	27	30	33	36
4	8	12	16	20	24	28	32	36	40	44	48
5	10	15	20	25	30	35	40	45	50	55	60
6	12	18	24	30	36	42	48	54	60	66	72
7	14	21	28	35	42	49	56	63	70	77	84
8	16	24	32	40	48	56	64	72	80	88	96
9	18	27	36	45	54	63	72	81	90	99	108
10	20	30	40	50	60	70	80	90	100	110	120
11	22	33	44	55	66	77	88	99	110	121	132
12	24	36	48	60	72	84	96	108	120	132	144

The Monthly Manager

Month of _____   Student's Name _____

	Monday	Tuesday	Wednesday	Thursday	Friday
Week of ____ to ____	B: I: R:	B: I: R:	B: I: R:	B: I: R:	B: I: R:
Week of ____ to ____	B: I: R:	B: I: R:	B: I: R:	B: I: R:	B: I: R:
Week of ____ to ____	B: I: R:	B: I: R:	B: I: R:	B: I: R:	B: I: R:
Week of ____ to ____	B: I: R:	B: I: R:	B: I: R:	B: I: R:	B: I: R:
Week of ____ to ____	B: I: R:	B: I: R:	B: I: R:	B: I: R:	B: I: R:

B = Behavior   I = Intervention   R = Result

Report Card

Key
C = Consistent   N = Needs Help
P = Progressing   / = Does Not Apply

Student: _____

Teacher: _____

Grade: _____

Report Period: _____

Spelling

Level: _____

Program: _____

Progress:	C	P	N	/
Effort:	C	P	N	/

Comments: _____

_____

Listening

Follows Directions:	C	P	N	/
Shows Understanding:	C	P	N	/
Enjoys Stories:	C	P	N	/

Comments: _____

_____

Speaking

Expresses Self Clearly:	C	P	N	/
Uses Good Diction:	C	P	N	/
Joins Discussions:	C	P	N	/

Comments: _____

_____

Writing

Writes Interesting Leads:	C	P	N	/
Sequences Ideas:	C	P	N	/
Develops Theme:	C	P	N	/
Uses "Voice" in Story:	C	P	N	/
Uses Grammatical Rules:	C	P	N	/
Uses Legible Penmanship:	C	P	N	/
Writes Strong Endings:	C	P	N	/

Comments: _____

_____

Social/Emotional Growth

Is Cooperative:	C	P	N	/
Accepts Responsibility:	C	P	N	/
Accepts Rules and Limits:	C	P	N	/
Uses Self-Control:	C	P	N	/

Comments: _____

_____

Reading

Level: _____

Program: _____

Selects Books at Level:	C	P	N	/
Reads Independently:	C	P	N	/
Reads for Meaning:	C	P	N	/
Self-Corrects:	C	P	N	/
Shows Understanding:	C	P	N	/
Sustains Silent Reading:	C	P	N	/
Enjoys Reading:	C	P	N	/
Reads Different Genres:	C	P	N	/

Comments: _____

_____

Math Concepts

Approximate Level: _____

Number Facts:	C	P	N	/
Number Sense:	C	P	N	/
Addition:	C	P	N	/
Subtraction:	C	P	N	/
Multiplication:	C	P	N	/
Division:	C	P	N	/
Geometry:	C	P	N	/
Measurement:	C	P	N	/
Problem Solving:	C	P	N	/

Comments: _____

_____

Social Studies/Science

Themes: _____

Participates:	C	P	N	/
Understands Concepts:	C	P	N	/
Effort:	C	P	N	/

Comments: _____

_____

Study and Work Habits

Stays on Task:	C	P	N	/
Completes Assignments:	C	P	N	/
Works Neatly:	C	P	N	/
Works Independently:	C	P	N	/
Stays Organized:	C	P	N	/

Comments: _____

_____

Resources

Assessment

Bridges, Lois. *Assessment: Continuous Learning*. Portland, ME: Stenhouse Publishers, 1996.

Brookhart, Susan. *Formative Assessment Strategies for Every Classroom*. Alexandria, VA: ASCD, 2006.

_____ . "Feedback That Fits." *Educational Leadership*, vol. 65, no. 4, December 2007/January 2008.

_____ . *How to Give Effective Feedback to Your Students*. Alexandria, VA: ASCD, 2008.

Dodge, Judith. *25 Quick Formative Assessments*. New York: Scholastic Professional Books, 2009.

Fiderer, Adele. *35 Rubrics & Checklists to Assess Reading and Writing: Time-Saving Reproducible Forms for Meaningful Literacy Assessment.* New York: Scholastic Professional Books, 1998.

Fisher, Douglas, and Nancy Frey. *The Formative Assessment Action Plan*. Alexandria, VA: ASCD, 2011.

Greenstein, Laura. *What Teachers Really Need to Know About Formative Assessment*. Alexandria, VA: ASCD, 2010.

Guskey, Thomas. "The Rest of the Story." *Educational Leadership*, vol. 65, no. 4, December 2007/January 2008.

_____ . "Lessons of Mastery Learning." *Educational Leadership*, vol. 68, no. 2, October 2010.

Hume, Karen. *Start Where They Are*. Toronto, Ontario: Pearson Canada, 2008.

_____ . *Evidence to Action*. Toronto, Ontario: Pearson Canada, 2009.

Jackson, Robyn. *Never Work Harder Than Your Students*. Alexandria, VA: ASCD, 2009.

_____ . "Flagged for Success." *Educational Leadership*, vol. 68, no. 2, October 2010.

Lazear, David. *Multiple Intelligence Approaches to Assessment: Solving the Assessment Conundrum*. Palatine, IL: IRI/Skylight Publishing, 1994.

MacDonald, Sharon. *Portfolio and Its Use: A Road Map for Assessment* (Book II). Little Rock, AR: Southern Early Childhood Association, 1996.

Marzano, Robert. *Classroom Assessment and Grading That Work*. Alexandria, VA: ASCD, 2006.

_____ . "When Students Track Their Progress." *Educational Leadership*, vol. 67, no. 4, December 2009/ January 2010.

_____ . "Reviving Reteaching." *Educational Leadership*, vol. 68, no. 2, October 2010.

Moss, Connie, and Susan Brookhart. *Advancing Formative Assessment in Every Classroom*. Alexandria, VA: ASCD, 2009.

O'Connor, Ken. A *Repair Kit for Grading: 15 Fixes for Broken Grades*. Portland, OR: Educational Testing Service, 2007.

Popham, W. James. *Transformative Assessment.* Alexandria, VA: ASCD, 2008.

Power, Brenda Miller. *Taking Note: Improving Your Observational Notetaking*. Portland, ME: Stenhouse Publishers, 1996.

_____ , and Kelly Chandler. *Well-Chosen Words: Narrative Assessments and Report Card Comments*. Portland, ME: Stenhouse Publishers, 1998.

Schipper, Beth, and Joanne Rossi. *Portfolios in the Classroom: Tools for Learning and Instruction*. Portland, ME: Stenhouse Publishers, 1997.

Stiggins, Richard J. *The Unfulfilled Promise of Classroom Assessment.* Portland, OR: Assessment Training Institute, 2001.

———. "Assessment Crisis: The Absence of Assessment for Learning." *Phi Delta Kappa*, vol. 83, no. 10, June 2002.

Strickland, Cindy. *Professional Development for Differentiating Instruction*. Alexandria, VA: ASCD, 2009.

Classroom Management and Discipline

Albert, Linda. *A Teacher's Guide to Cooperative Discipline.* Circle Pines, MN: American Guidance Service, 1989.

Nelson, Jane, Lynn Lott, and Stephen Glenn. *Positive Discipline in the Classroom*. Rocklin, CA: Prima Publishing, 2000.

Whyte, Donna. *You Can't Teach a Class You Can't Manage*. Peterborough, NH: Crystal Springs Books, 2008.

Wong, Harry. T*he First Days of School: How to Be an Effective Teacher.* Mountain View, CA: Harry K. Wong Publications, 1998.

Developmental Education/Readiness

Brazelton, T. Berry. *Touchpoints*. Reading, MA: Perseus Books, 1992.

———. *The Irreducible Needs of Children*. Reading, MA: Addison-Wesley, 2001.

Grant, Jim, and Bob Johnson. *Readiness Checklist for Kindergarten*. Peterborough, NH: Crystal Springs Books, 1997.

Kraus, Robert. *Leo the Late Bloomer*. New York: Harper-Collins, 1971.

Wood, Chip. *Yardsticks: Children in the Classroom Ages 4–14*. Greenfield, MA: Northeast Foundation for Children, 1997.

Differentiated Instruction

Beninghof, Anne M. *Engage All Students Through Differentiation*. Peterborough, NH: Crystal Springs Books, 2006.

Cash, Richard. *Advancing Differentiation*. Minneapolis, MN: Free Spirit Publishing, 2011.

Forsten, Char, Gretchen Goodman, Jim Grant, Betty Hollas, and Donna Whyte. *The More Ways You Teach, the More Students You Reach*. Peterborough, NH: Crystal Springs Books, 2006.

Goodman, Gretchen. *Interventions for Struggling Learners*. Peterborough, NH: Crystal Springs Books, 2008.

Gregory, Gayle H., and Carolyn Chapman. *Differentiated Instructional Strategies*. Thousand Oaks, CA: Corwin Press, 2002.

Heacox, Diane. *Differentiating Instruction in the Regular Classroom*. Minneapolis, MN: Free Spirit Publishing, 2002.

———. *Making Differentiation a Habit*. Minneapolis, MN: Free Spirit Publishing, 2008.

Hollas, Betty. *Differentiating Instruction in a Whole-Group Setting* (Grades 3–8). Peterborough, NH: Crystal Springs Books, 2005.

————. *Differentiating Instruction in a Whole-Group Setting* (Grades 7–12). Peterborough, NH: Crystal Springs Books, 2007.

————, with Char Forsten, Jim Grant, and Laureen Reynolds. *Question-Answer Relationships*. Peterborough, NH: Crystal Springs Books, 2008.

Marzano. Robert. "Using Games to Enhance Achievement." *Educational Leadership*. February 2010.

Tomlinson, Carol Ann. *The Differentiated Classroom: Responding to the Needs of All Learners*. Alexandria, VA: ASCD, 1999.

————. *Leadership for Differentiating Schools and Classrooms*. Alexandria, VA: ASCD, 2000.

————. *How to Differentiate Instruction in Mixed-Ability Classrooms.* 2nd ed. Alexandria, VA: ASCD, 2001.

————, and Marcia B. Imbeau. *Leading and Managing a Differentiated Classroom*. Alexandria, VA: ASCD, 2010.

VanderWeide, Donna. *Different Tools for Different Learners*. Peterborough, NH: Crystal Springs Books, 2004.

————. *Differentiated Math.* Peterborough, NH: Crystal Springs Books, 2008.

Winebrenner, Susan. T*eaching Gifted Kids in the Regular Classroom*. Minneapolis, MN: Free Spirit Publishing, 2002.

Wormeli, Rick. *Fair Isn't Always Equal*. Portland, ME: Stenhouse Publishers, 2006.

————. *Differentiation: From Planning to Practice*. Portland, ME: Stenhouse Publishers, 2007.

Issues in Education

Barrs, Myra, and Sue Pidgeon, eds. *Gender and Reading in Elementary Classrooms*. Portland, ME: Stenhouse Publishers, 1994.

Payne, Ruby K., Ph.D. *Poverty: A Framework for Understanding and Working with Students and Adults from Poverty*. 4th ed. Highlands, TX: aha! Process, Inc., 2005.

Wortman, Robert. *Administrators Supporting School Change*. Portland, ME: Stenhouse Publishers, 1995.

Learning Centers

Allen, Irene, and Susan Peery. *Literacy Centers: What Your Other Kids Do During Guided Reading Groups*. Cypress, CA: Creative Teaching Press, 2000.

Feldman, Jean. *Transition Time: Let's Do Something Different!* Beltsville, MD: Gryphon House, 1995.

————. *Wonderful Rooms Where Children Can Bloom!* 2nd ed. Peterborough, NH: Crystal Springs Books, 2011.

Finney, Susan. *Keep the Rest of the Class Reading and Writing . . . While You Teach Small Groups* (Grades 3–6). New York: Scholastic Professional Books, 2000.

MacDonald, Sharon. S*quish, Sort, Paint, and Build: Over 200 Easy Learning Center Activities*. Beltsville, MD: Gryphon House, 1996.

Marriott, Donna. *What Are the Other Kids Doing . . . While You Teach Small Groups?* Cypress, CA: Creative Teaching Press, 1997.

Morrow, Lesley Mandel. *The Literacy Center: Contexts for Reading and Writing*. Portland, ME: Stenhouse Publishers, 2002.

Learning Strategies/Multiple Intelligences

Armstrong, Thomas. *Multiple Intelligences in the Classroom*. Alexandria, VA: ASCD, 1994.

Campbell, Linda, Bruce Campbell, and Dee Dickinson. T*eaching and Learning Through Multiple Intelligences*. 3rd ed. Needham Heights, MA: Allyn & Bacon, 2003.

Gardner, Howard. *Frames of Mind: The Theory of Multiple Intelligences.* New York: Basic Books, 1985.

————. *Multiple Intelligences: The Theory in Practice*. New York: Basic Books, 1990.

————. *The Unschooled Mind: How Children Think and How Schools Should Teach*. New York: Basic Books, 1990.

Jensen, Eric. *Super Teaching, Turning Point*. San Diego, CA: The Brain Store, 1995.

————. *Introduction to Brain-Compatible Learning*. San Diego, CA: The Brain Store, 1998.

————. *Brain Compatible Strategies*. San Diego, CA: The Brain Store, 2004.

————. *Teaching with the Brain in Mind* (K–6). Alexandria, VA: ASCD, 1998.

Lazear, David. *Eight Ways of Knowing: Teaching for Multiple Intelligences*. 3rd ed. Thousand Oaks, CA: Corwin Press, 1999.

Payne, Ruby K., Ph.D. *Poverty: A Framework for Understanding and Working with Students and Adults from Poverty*. 4th ed. Highlands, TX: aha! Process, Inc, 2005.

Short, Kathy G., Jean Schroder, Julie Laird, Gloria Kauffman, Margaret J. Ferguson, and Kathleen Marie Crawford. *Learning Together Through Inquiry: From Columbus to Integrated Curriculum.* Portland, ME: Stenhouse Publishers, 1996.

Wolfe, Pat, Ph.D. *Brain Matters: Translating Brain Research into Classroom Practice*. Alexandria, VA: ASCD, 1996.

Math

Coates, Grace Davila, and Jean Kerr Stenmark. *Family Math for Young Children*. Berkeley, CA: Lawrence Hall of Science, University of California at Berkeley, 1997.

Crooks, Lisa. *Munchable Math*. Huntington Beach, CA: Creative Teaching Press, 2000.

Currah, Joanne, et al. *All Hands on Deck*. Edmonton, Alberta: Box Cars and One-Eyed Jacks, 1997.

Dienes, Zoltan. *Building Up Mathematics*. London: Hutchison Educational Limited, 1971.

Gibbons, Pauline. *Scaffolding Language, Scaffolding Learning*. Portsmouth, NH: Heinemann, 2002.

Goodnow, Judy, et al. *The Problem Solver Series and Materials* (Grades 1–8). Bothell, WA: Creative Publications, 1988.

Keene, Ellin, and Susan Zimmerman. *Mosaic of Thought: The Power of Comprehension Strategy Instruction*. 2nd ed. Portsmouth, NH: Heinemann, 2007.

Kuhns, Catherine Jones. *Building Number Sense*. Peterborough, NH: Crystal Springs Books, 2009.

Lee, Martin, and Marcia Miller. *5-Minute Math Problem of the Day* (Grades 4–8). New York: Scholastic Professional Books, 2000.

Lee, Peng Yee, ed. *Teaching Primary School Mathematics*. Singapore: McGraw-Hill, 2007.

Leinwand, Steven. *Accessible Mathematics*. Portsmouth, NH: Heinemann, 2009.

Long, Lynette. *Marvelous Multiplication*. New York: John Wiley and Sons, 2000.

Pappas, Theoni. *Fractals, Googols, and Other Mathematical Tales*. San Carlos, CA: Wide World Publishing, 1993.

Parker, Thomas H., and Scott J. Baldridge. *Elementary Mathematics for Teachers*. Bloomington, IN: Sefton-Ash Publishing, 2003.

Skemp, Richard. *Mathematics in the Primary School*. London: Routledge Falmer, 2002.

Stenmark, Jean Kerr, Virginia Thompson, and Ruth Cossey. *Family Math*. Berkeley, CA: Lawrence Hall of Science, 1986.

Van de Walle, John A., Karen S. Karp, and Jennifer M. Bay-Williams. *Elementary and Middle School Mathematics: Teaching Developmentally*. 7th ed. San Francisco: Allyn & Bacon, 2010.

Vydra, Joan, and Jean McCall. *No Problem!* San Luis Obispo, CA: Dandy Lion, 1989.

Vygotsky, Lev S. *Mind in Society: The Development of Higher Psychological Processes*. London: Harvard University Press, 1978.

Math-Related Children's Books

Burns, Marilyn. *The Greedy Triangle*. New York: Scholastic Paperbacks, 2008.

Scieszka, Jon, and Lane Smith. *Math Curse*. New York: Viking, 1995.

Viorst, Judith. Alexander, *Who Used to Be Rich Last Sunday*. New York: Atheneum Books for Young Readers, 2009.

Parent Involvement/Resources for Parents

Fassler, David, and Lynne S. Dumas. *Help Me, I'm Sad*. New York: Putnam Penguin, 1997.

Summer Bridge Series. Salt Lake City, UT: Rainbow Bridge Publishing.

Vopat, James. *The Parent Project: A Workshop Approach to Parent Involvement*. Portland, ME: Stenhouse Publishers, 1994.

Reading, Writing, Spelling, and Vocabulary

Allen, Janet. *Words, Words, Words: Teaching Vocabulary in Grades 4–12*. Portland, ME: Stenhouse Publishers, 1999.

———. *Yellow Brick Roads: Shared and Guided Paths to Independent Reading 4–12*. Portland, ME: Stenhouse Publishers, 2000.

Allen, Margaret. *The Dr. Maggie Classroom Phonics Kit*. Cypress, CA: Creative Teaching Press, 1999.

———. *Dr. Maggie's Phonics Readers: A New View for PreK–2*. Cypress, CA: Creative Teaching Press, 1999.

———. *Dr. Maggie's Phonics Resource Guide (PreK–2)*. Cypress, CA: Creative Teaching Press, 1999.

Atwell, Nancie, ed. *Coming to Know: Writing to Learn in the Intermediate Grades.* Portsmouth, NH: Heinemann, 1990.

Billmeyer, Rachel, and Mary Lee Barton. *Teaching Reading in the Content Areas*. Aurora, CO: McRel, 1998.

Blotcher, Wendy. *Success with Sight Words* (1–3). Huntington Beach, CA: Creative Teaching Press, 1999.

Buehl, Doug. *Classroom Strategies for Interactive Learning*. Newark, DE: International Reading Association, 2001.

Carbo, Marie. *What Every Principal Should Know About Teaching Reading: How to Raise Test Scores and Nurture a Love of Reading*. Syosset, NY: National Learning Styles Institute, 1997.

Chambers, Aidan. T*ell Me: Children, Reading, and Talk*. Portland, ME: Stenhouse Publishers, 1996.

Cunningham, Patricia M., and Dorothy P. Hall. *Making Big Words: Multilevel, Hands-On Spelling and Phonics Activities* (Grades 3–6). Torrance, CA: Good Apple, 1994.

Dorn, Linda J., Cathy French, and Tammy Jones. *Apprenticeship in Literacy: Transitions Across Reading and Writing*. Portland, ME: Stenhouse Publishers, 1998.

Fitzpatrick, Jo. *Solving Writing Problems* (2–4). Huntington Beach, CA: Creative Teaching Press, 1999.

———— . *Teaching Beginning Writing* (K–2). Huntington Beach, CA: Creative Teaching Press, 1999.

Fountas, Irene C., and Gay Su Pinnell. *Guided Reading: Good First Teaching for All Children*. Portsmouth, NH: Heinemann, 1996.

———— . *Guiding Readers and Writers (Grades 3–6): Teaching Comprehension, Genre, and Content Literacy*. Portsmouth, NH: Heinemann, 2001.

Fry, Edward, Ph.D. *1000 Instant Words*. Laguna Beach, CA: Laguna Beach Educational Books, 1994.

———— . *Dr. Fry's Phonics: Onset and Rime Word Lists*. Laguna Beach, CA: Laguna Beach Educational Books, 1994.

———— . *How to Teach Reading*. Laguna Beach, CA: Laguna Beach Educational Books, 1995.

Harvey, Stephanie. *Nonfiction Matters: Reading, Writing, and Research in Grades 3–8*. Portland, ME: Stenhouse Publishers, 1998.

———— , and Anne Goudvis. *Strategies That Work*. Portland, ME: Stenhouse Publishers, 2000.

Heller, Ruth. *Kites Sail High: And Other Books on Nouns, Adjectives, and Adverbs*. New York: Paper Star, 1998.

Hong, Min, and Patsy Stafford. *Spelling Strategies That Work: Practical Ways to Motivate Students to Become Successful Spellers* (Grades K–2). New York: Scholastic Professional Books, 1997.

Hoyt, Linda. *Revisit, Reflect, Retell: Time-Tested Strategies for Teaching Reading Comprehension*. Portsmouth, NH: Heinemann, 2009.

Irvin, Judith. *Reading and the Middle School Student*. Boston: Allyn & Bacon, 1998.

Keene, Ellin, and Susan Zimmerman. *Mosaic of Thought: The Power of Comprehension Strategy Instruction*. 2nd ed. Portsmouth, NH: Heinemann, 2007.

Lapin, Gloria. *Sight Word Stories: Alternate Strategies for Emergent Readers*. Torrance, CA: Fearon Teacher Aids, 1997.

Lynch, Judy. *Easy Lessons for Teaching Word Families* (Grades K–2). New York: Scholastic Professional Books, 1998.

Mader, Carol. *Vowels: Phonics Without Worksheets*. Huntington Beach, CA: Creative Teaching Press, 1999.

Marzano, Robert, Debra J. Pickering, and Jane Pollack. *Classroom Instruction That Works: Research-Based Strategies for Increasing Student Achievement*. Alexandria, VA: ASCD, 2001.

Moen, Christine. *20 Reproducible Literature Circle Role Sheets* (Grades 1–3). Dayton, OH: Teaching & Learning Company, 2000.

Nickelsen, LeAnn. *Quick Activities to Build a Very Voluminous Vocabulary* (Grades 4–8). New York: Scholastic Professional Books, 1998.

Opitz, Michael. F*lexible Grouping in Reading* (Grades 2–5). New York: Scholastic Professional Books, 1998.

————, and Timothy Rasinski. *Good-Bye Round Robin: 25 Effective Oral Reading Strategies.* Updated edition. Portsmouth, NH: Heinemann, 2008.

Raphael, Taffy. "Question-Answer Strategy for Children." *The Reading Teacher*, 36, 303–311, 1982.

Samway, Katharine Davies, and Gail Whang. *Literature Study Circles in a Multicultural Classroom*. Portland, ME: Stenhouse Publishers, 1995.

Stephens, Elaine C., and Jean E. Brown. *A Handbook of Content Literacy Strategies: 75 Practical Reading and Writing Ideas*. Norwood, MA: Christopher Gordon Publishers, 2000.

Stitt, Neil. T*ake Any Book: Hundreds of Activities to Develop Basic Learning Skills Using Any Book*. Torrance, CA: Fearon Teacher Aids, 1998.

Szymusiak, Karen, and Franki Sibberson. *Beyond Leveled Books: Supporting Transitional Readers in Grades 2–5*. Portland, ME: Stenhouse Publishers, 2001.

Team Teaching. The Northern Nevada Writing Project Teacher-Researcher Group. Portland, ME: Stenhouse Publishers, 1996.

Tovani, Cris. *I Read It, but I Don't Get It: Comprehension Strategies for Adolescent Readers*. Portland, ME: Stenhouse Publishers, 2000.

Zgonc, Yvette. *Interventions for All: Phonological Awareness*. Peterborough, NH: Crystal Springs Books, 2010.

Social Studies and Science

Edinger, Monica, and Stephanie Fins. *Far Away and Long Ago: Young Historians in the Classroom*. Portland, ME: Stenhouse Publishers, 1998.

Julio, Susan. *Great Map Mysteries: 18 Stories and Maps to Build Geography and Map Skills* (Grades 3–6). New York: Scholastic Professional Books, 1997.

Kohl, MaryAnn, and Jean Potter. *Science Arts: Discovering Science Through Art Experiences*. Bellingham, WA: Bright Ring Publishing, 1993.

MacDonald, Sharon. *Everyday Discoveries: Amazingly Easy Science and Math Using Stuff You Already Have*. Beltsville, MD: Gryphon House, 1998.

Ruef, Kerry. *Looking/Thinking by Analogy: A Guide to Developing the Interdisciplinary Mind*. Seattle, WA: The Private Eye Project, 1992.

Steffey, Stephanie, and Wendy J. Hood, eds. *If This Is Social Studies, Why Isn't It Boring?* Portland, ME: Stenhouse Publishers, 1994.

Special Education, Attention Deficit Disorder (ADD)/Attention Deficit Hyperactivity Disorder (ADHD), and Other Disorders

Atwood, Tony. *Asperger's Syndrome*. Philadelphia, PA: Jessica Kingsley Publishers, 1998.

Brohl, Kathryn. *Working with Traumatized Children: A Handbook for Healing*. Washington, DC: Child Welfare League of America, 2007.

Irlen, Helen. *Reading by the Colors: Overcoming Dyslexia and Other Reading Disabilities Through the Irlen Method*. Updated ed. New York: Berkeley Publishing Group Inc., 2005.

Nowicki, Stephen, and Marshall P. Duke. *Helping the Child Who Doesn't Fit In*. Atlanta, GA: Peachtree Publishers, 1992.

Tracking/Untracking

George, Paul. *How to Untrack Your School*. Alexandria, VA: ASCD, 1992.

Kohn, Alfie. *No Contest: The Case Against Competition*. Boston: Houghton Mifflin, 1992.

Oakes, Jeannie. *Keeping Track: How Schools Structure Inequality*. 2nd ed. New Haven, CT: Yale University Press, 2005.

Wheelock, Anne. *Crossing the Tracks: How "Untracking" Can Save America's Schools*. New York: New Press, 1993.

Websites

Ask Eric Virtual Library: eric.ed.gov

Crystal Springs Books: sde.com/crystalsprings

Interact: interact-simulations.com

readinglady.com

Staff Development for Educators: sde.com

teachnet.com

Publishers and Distributors of Recommended Math Books and Products

Creative Publications, Inc.
5623 W 115th Street
Alsip, IL 60482
708-385-0400

Crystal Springs Books
10 Sharon Road, PO Box 500
Peterborough, NH 03458-0500
800-321-0401
sde.com/crystalsprings

ETA/Cuisenaire
500 Greenview Court
Vernon Hills, IL 60061
800-445-5985

National Council of Teachers of Mathematics
1906 Association Drive
Reston, VA 20191-1502
800-235-7566
nctm.org

SingaporeMath.com Inc.
404 Beavercreek Road, #225
Oregon City, OR 97045
503-557-8100
singaporemath.com

Index

A

ABCYA website, 35, 39

Acetate strips. *See* Highlighting strips or tape

Acronyms: for learning in bite-size chunks, 64; as mnemonic device, 54

ActivExpression by Promethean website, 108

Activity sheets, page protectors for, 50

ADD/ADHD, resources on, 152–53

Adding-machine tape, for Personal-Learning Time Lines, 111

Addition facts, playing cards for practicing, 90

Addition problems: grid for, *139*; separating, from subtraction problems, 97

Advertising for one's own replacement, for community building, 33

Airplane headphone, for parallel reading, 41

Airplanes, paper, for conveying praise, 31

Allergies, food, 89, *137–38*

Anchor activities: charts for choosing, 8; for math practice, 100, 101

Anecdotal Records, for tracking success of interventions, 107, *144*

Animals: for name-tag activity, 22; stuffed, telling problems to, 1; website on, 8

Animoto website, 57

Applications, online sources for, 42

Apply a Different Symbol System, as literacy strategy, 75

Appointments, with Clock Partners activity, 26, *127*

Appreciation Circle, for community building, 23

Artwork, eliminating distracting, as literacy strategy, 56

Assessment resources, 146–47

Assessment strategies: alternative kind of report card, 114, *145*; anecdotal records for tracking success of interventions, 107, *144*; chart game for review, 118; curriculum compacting and, vii–viii; ensuring correct practice in math and spelling, 110; exit slips on online sticky notes, 119; flash-card game for review, 115; game playing, 39; journaling about personal learning, 111; polling students with hand-held wireless response devices, 108; response cards, 106; rubrics, 116; separating language from computation in math papers, 109; student-led conferences, 113; surveys, 117; video recordings, 112

B

Attention deficit disorder (ADD)/attention deficit hyperactivity disorder (ADHD), resources on, 152–53

Attention problems, help for students with, 41, 49, 55

Attitude, self-talk for improving, 9

Auditory processing of information, eye directionality indicating, 10

Averages, finding, 105, *130*

Behavior patterns, anecdotal records for tracking, 107, *144*

Behavior problems: classroom seating for students with, 2; Popsicle sticks as tool for correcting, 14

Bingo chips: for computing averages, 105; as math counters, 38

Bite-size chunks, for presenting concepts, 64

Blindfold, for demonstrating interdependence, 30

Books: math, publishers and distributors of, 154; timely, for educators, 153

Box One, Circle the Other, as math strategy, 97

Brain Compatible Strategies, 10

BrainPOP website, 52

Brain's midline, determining ability to cross, 63

Bring It into Focus, as literacy strategy, 59, *133*

Build Your Wild Self website, 8

Bulletin board, online, for posting student responses, 119

Buried letters, as mnemonic device, 54

Business cards, for identifying student experts, 25

Buzz Sheet questions, for mixer activity, 32, *129*

C

Calculations in a Zip, as math strategy, 86

Calendars: for finding averages, 105; online, for planning presentations, 18

Calling All Numbers, as math strategy, 100

Camera, digital, for learning math concepts, 91

Can You Spot the Learning?, focusing tools in, 45

C.A.P.S. Off to Editing, as literacy strategy, 66

Capture Math Facts with Captive Dice, 93

Cards, playing, for math games, 90

Carrel, desk, for avoiding visual distractions, 3

Catch That Word, for focusing attention, 49

Cell phones, podcasting using, 18

Note: Page numbers in italics indicate reproducibles to be used with strategies.

Charts: for choosing anchor activities, 8; Dueling, for review, 118; for Facts in a Flash game, 115; finger pointer used with, 48; using highlighting tape with, 43

Choice Charts, for finding anchor activities, 8

Classroom Buzz, The, as mixer activity, 32, *129*

Classroom management and discipline resources, 147

Classroom seating locations, 2

Class Walkway, for encouraging students facing difficulties, 20

Clickers, for assessment, 108

Clock, analog, telling time on, 94

Clock Partners, appointment making with, 26, *127*

Colorful Questions, as literacy strategy, 76

Colors, for correcting assignments, 5

Comic Master website, 61

Comic strips: creating, as after-reading activity, 61; for learning in bite-size chunks, 64

Community-building strategies: advertising for one's own replacement, 33; animal name-tag activity, 22; appreciation circle, 23; avoiding negative messages, 21; blindfold activity for demonstrating interdependence, 30; business cards to identify student experts, 25; Classroom Buzz mixer activity, 32, *129*; clock partners for making appointments, 26, *127*; identifying common interests with "I have never" game, 34; mix-it activity for promoting group interaction, 27; online games and activities, 19; paper airplanes for conveying praise, 31; praise-behind-your-back activity, 24; scavenger hunt for identifying multiple intelligences, 29; toothpaste demonstration for encouraging respectful communication, 28; walkway for encouraging students facing difficulties, 20

Community Puzzles, for group projects, 12

Community study, group projects on, viii, 12

Computation errors, preventing, 98, *139–42*

Conferences, Student-Led, as assessment strategy, 113

Corkboard website, 119

Correcting assignments, marker colors for, 5

C.P.S.R. (Copy-Pair-Share-Respond), as literacy strategy, 74, *136*

Crayola Digi-Color website, 8

Creaza Education website, 61

Cross the Midline, as literacy strategy, 63

Cross Out Every Other Math Example, 99

Curriculum compacting, vii–viii

D

Definitions, embedded, as mnemonic device, 54

Desk carrel, for avoiding visual distractions, 3

Developmental education/readiness resources, 147

Dice, for practicing math facts, 93

Differentiated instruction: global strategies associated with, vii–viii; meaning of, vii; resources on, 147–48

Digital camera, for learning math concepts, 91

Digital comic strips, creating, as after-reading activity, 61

Digital photo books, for presentations, 18

Digital R.A.F.T., as literacy strategy, 65

Digital Scavenger Hunts, as literacy strategy, 82

Discipline resources, 147

Discouraged students. *See also* Struggling students: help for, 2, 9, 87, 99

Discovery Puzzlemaker website, 8

Disruptive students, seating location encouraging, 2

Distractions, avoiding: with desk carrel, 3; with ear protection, 55; with focus frames, 46, *131*; with large print and less artwork, 56; from music, 23; with seating location, 2; with vocal immersion, 41

Division facts, highlighting strips for learning, 102

Division/multiplication relationships, factors reinforcing, 104

Division problems: graph paper for, 98; grid for, *142*

Drawing website, 8

Dueling Charts, as assessment strategy, 118

E

Ear protection, for distracted students, 55

Editing: mnemonics for, 66; Post-It Notes for, 44

Education issues, resources on, 148

eInstruction website, 108

Embedded definitions, as mnemonic device, 54

Encore game, for reviewing concepts, 17

English language learners, help for, 9, 40, 75, 85, 102, 109

Enlarge Print and Eliminate Distracting Artwork, as literacy strategy, 56

Note: Page numbers in italics indicate reproducibles to be used with strategies.

EpiPen® instructions, for responding to food allergies, *138*

Equivalent Fractions Before Your Eyes, as math strategy, 103, *143*

eThemes website, 35

Exit slips, for assessment, 119

Experts, identifying student, 25

Eye directionality, providing instruction cues, 10

Eyes Have It, The!, indicating information processing, 10

F

Factoring numbers, 104

Facts in a Flash, as assessment strategy, 115

Familiarity Breeds Attempt, as literacy strategy, 58

Field trips, virtual, as literacy strategy, 69

Finding Your Voice, as literacy strategy, 62

Fine-motor difficulties, helping students with, 43, 51

Finger pointer, for nonverbal signaling, 48

First Things First: Cross the Midline, as literacy strategy, 63

Flash cards: for review game, 115; triangular, for reinforcing number-family relationships, 95; websites for creating, 8

Flexible grouping of students, viii

Flickr website, 91

FlipSnack website, 65

Flying High with Praise, for eliciting positive comments about students, 31

Focus frames, making, 46, *131*

Focusing on the Facts, as math strategy, 102

Focusing tools: focus frames, 46, *131*; highlighting tape (*see* Highlighting strips or tape); large print, 56; plastic insects, 45; Post-It Notes, 44; response cards, 106; sliding mask, 47, *132*; Sticky-Note Symbols, 80; word catcher, 49

Food Allergy Action Plan, 89, *137–38*

4-6-8, as literacy strategy, 68, *134*

Fractions, equivalent, 103, *143*

Framework for Understanding Poverty, A, 10

Freeology website, 18

Front and Center, for encouraging sitting in front of classroom, 2

Funneling Information, talking tube for, 40

Funny, Sunny Times, for introducing online games and activities, 19

G

Games: creating Word Maps, 70, *135*; Dueling Charts, for review, 118; Encore, for reviewing concepts, 17; flash-card, for review, 115; Human Scrabble, 60; "I have never," for identifying common interests, 34; instruction-giving, 16; math, 90, 92; Money Summary, for finding main idea in text, 83; online, 8, 19, 39; Three Facts and a Fib, 71

Get a Grip on It, for handwriting problems, 51

Get the Picture, as math strategy, 91

Ghoulie Games website, 19

Glogster website, 18

Goals for learning, setting, 111

Google Earth Showcase website, 69

Google Earth website, 69

Google Lit Trips website, 69

Go to the Mat for Learning, as math strategy, 88

Go Wild, as animal name-tag activity, 22

Grades: on alternative report cards, 114, *145*; response devices calculating, 108; written on Post-It Notes, 44

Graphic organizers: for digital scavenger hunts, 82; for planning presentations, 18

Grids: for avoiding careless computation errors, 98, *139–42*; for visualizing number patterns, 105

Group assignments, using puzzles for, 12

Grouping of students, flexible, viii

H

Hand-held wireless response devices, for assessment, 108

Hand Huggers, for handwriting problems, 51

Handwriting: "drifting," computation errors from, 98; tools for problems with, 51

Headbands, for vocabulary building, 77

Help Wanted, as signal for assistance, 13

Here's Looking at You, Kid, as alternative report card for assessment, 114, *145*

Higher-order thinking skills, digital comic strips for developing, 61

Highlighting strips or tape: for finding equivalent fractions on multiplication chart, 103; for finding key ideas, 43; for reinforcing multiplication and division facts, 102; used with large print, 56

Highlighting What's Important, 43

Note: Page numbers in italics indicate reproducibles to be used with strategies.

High-Tech Assessment, with video recordings, 112
Homework: establishing guidelines for, 7, *124*; watching video for, 52
Howdy, Partner Factor!, as math strategy, 104
Human Scrabble, as literacy strategy, 60
Hundreds Chart: for finding averages, 105, *130*; for finding numerical patterns, 38, *130*

I

"I Can" Slips, for recording student success, 15, *126*
iMovie website, 57
In Praise of Page Protectors, for work sheets or activity sheets, 50
Insects, plastic, as focusing tool, 45
Instructional game, student-to-student, 16
Instructions, helping struggling students with, 109
Integrated curriculum, avoiding confusion from, 64
Interactive whiteboard: finger pointer used with, 48; as learning center, 35; online games for, 39
Interdependence, blindfold activity demonstrating, 30
Interests, common, game for identifying, 34
Intervention Plan, for struggling students, 11, *125*
Interventions, anecdotal records for tracking success of, 107, *144*
In the News, as literacy strategy, 73
iPads, 42
iPods, 42
It's About Time, for teaching time orientation, 53
It's a Plan, for creating Intervention Plan for struggling students, 11, *125*
I've Got Time, as math strategy, 94

J

Jigsaw Planet website, 8
Jingles: for learning in bite-size chunks, 64; as mnemonic device, 54
Journaling: as after-reading activity, 74, *136*; about personal learning, 111; for recording positive self-talk, 9

K

Keep Your Numbers in Line, for avoiding careless computation errors, 98, *139–42*
Khan Academy website, 52
Kinesthetic learners, help for, 29, 37, 64, 75, 86

L

Large print, for improving student focus, 56
Learning center(s): interactive whiteboard as, 35; page protectors used in, 50; purpose of, viii; resources on, 148
Learning Games for Kids website, 8
Learning goals, setting, 111
Learning strategies, resources on, 149
Left-handed students: eye directionality in, 10; materials and tools for, 6, *123*
Left-handed supplies websites, 6
Left-Hander Factoids, 6, *123*
"Lefties" Have Different Needs, 6, *123*
Letters: buried, as mnemonic device, 54; for Human Scrabble, 60
Let the Games Begin, using online sources for, 39
Level the Playing Field, as assessment strategy, 109
Lights, Camera, Writing, as literacy strategy, 57
Listen to Yourself, for encouraging positive and procedural self-talk, 9
Literacy strategies: active involvement for vocabulary building, 75; bite-size chunks for presenting concepts, 64; color-coding questions, 76; C.P.S.R. journaling method, 74, *136*; creating digital comic strips, 61; determining ability to cross the brain's midline, 63; digital scavenger hunts, 82; enlarging print and eliminating distracting artwork, 56; 4-6-8 story-writing activity, 68, *134*; headbands for vocabulary building, 77; Human Scrabble, 60; improving comprehension when reading aloud, 62; mnemonic for editing, 66; Money Summary for finding main idea in text, 83; movie or slide show production, 57; overlays for Scotopic Sensitivity Syndrome, 59, *133*; partner pairing for reading fluency, 78; pass-alongs to encourage independent reading, 79; pre-teaching new or difficult concepts, 58; question cards for building connections, 85; reading news articles, 73; splash-and-sort prereading activity, 72; sticky notes for responding to text, 80; summarizing reading passages, 84; true/false game, 71; virtual field trips, 69; windowpaning favorite story scenes, 81; word clouds for vocabulary building, 67; word map for vocabulary building, 70, *135*; writing from perspectives other than own, 65

Note: Page numbers in italics indicate reproducibles to be used with strategies.

Little Bird Tales website, 65

Low-income students, time orientation problems of, 53

M

Magic 20, as literacy strategy, 84

Magnetic bingo chips, as math counters, 38

Magnetic Poetry website, 8

Main idea in text: game for finding, 83; highlighting, 43

Management resources, 147

Management strategies: desk carrel for avoiding visual distractions, 3; encouraging sitting in front of classroom, 2; establishing homework guidelines, 7, *124*; eye directionality providing instruction cues, 10; finding anchor activities with Choice Charts, 8; "Help Wanted" sign to ask for assistance, 13; "I CAN" can, for focusing on student success, 15, *126*; Intervention Plan for struggling students, 11, *125*; music in classroom, 4; picking presentation style for research projects, 18; Popsicle sticks with student names, 14; positive and procedural self-talk, 9; problem reporting, 1, *122*; processing what's been learned, 17; puzzles for assigning group projects, 12; student-to-student instructional game, 16; tools for left-handed students, 6, *123*; yellow markers for highlighting answers, 5

Manage with Music, for classroom atmosphere, 4

Manage with Popsicle Sticks, for calling on students, 14

Manga High website, 39

Mark with the Sunshine, for correcting assignments, 5

Math counters, bingo chips as, 38

Math facts: dice for practicing, 93; highlighting strips for reinforcing, 102; name tags for reinforcing, 96; page protectors for practicing, 50; place mats for practicing, 88; playing cards for practicing, 90

Math games, online, 39

Math problems: crossing out every other, for reducing workload, 99; highlighting to signal need for reworking, 5; Post-It Notes for focusing on, 44; separating language from computation in, 109

Math-related children's books, 150

Math resources, 149–50

Math Snacks website, 39

Math strategies: for avoiding careless computation errors, 98, *139–42*; for avoiding confusion in mixed-operation problems, 97; cutting math papers into strips, 87; digital camera or images for learning concepts, 91; edibles for teaching concepts, 89, *137–38*; ensuring correct math practice, 110; factoring numbers to reinforce multiplication/division relationships, 104; finding averages, 105, *130*; highlighting strips used with multiplication charts, 102, *143*; modifying workload for discouraged learners, 99; multiplication chart for finding equivalent fractions, 103, *143*; name tags for reinforcing math facts, 96; newspapers for math practice, 101; number relationships game, 92; phone book pages for math practice, 100; place mats for math-facts practice, 88; presorting playing cards to match skill levels, 90; separating word problems from basic math examples, 109; storing dice for math-facts practice, 93; telling time, 86, 94; triangular flash cards for reinforcing number-family relationships, 95; zipper for, 86

Memorize with Mnemonics, 54

Mentoring, viii

Midline of brain, determining ability to cross, 63

Misbehavior. *See* Behavior problems

Mixbook website, 18

Mixed operations in math problems, 97

Mix It, Mix It, for promoting group interaction, 27

Mnemonics: for editing, 66; types of, 54

Mobile devices, as teaching tool, 42

Money Summary, as literacy strategy, 83

Monthly Manager, The, for tracking success of interventions, 107, *144*

Mouse Mischief website, 108

Movie Maker website, 57

Movie production, as literacy strategy, 57

Multiple intelligences: resources on, 149; vocabulary building and, 75

Multiple Intelligence Scavenger Hunt, 29, *128*

Multiplication Chart: for finding averages, 105; for finding equivalent fractions, 103, *143*; highlighting strips used with, 102

Note: Page numbers in italics indicate reproducibles to be used with strategies.

Multiplication/division relationships, factors reinforcing, 104

Multiplication facts, playing cards for practicing, 90

Multiplication practice, in learning centers, viii

Multiplication problems, grid for, *141*

Music: for Appreciation Circle, 23; for classroom management, 4; for Flying High with Praise activity, 31; used with writing activity, 17; websites on, 8

N

Names of students, on Popsicle sticks, 14

Name tags: animal, for community building, 22; for reinforcing math facts, 96

NCTE Read Write Think website, 61

Negative messages, avoiding, 9, 21

Negative numbers, zipper for learning, 86

Netbooks, 42

News articles, reading, as literacy strategy, 73

Newseum website, 73

Newspaper in Education website, 73

Newspapers, for math practice, 101

New York Philharmonic website, 8

No Can'ts Allowed, for focusing on student success, 15, *126*

Nonverbal signaling, with finger pointer, 48

No Problem!, for problem reporting, 1, *122*

Not Your Average Math Practice, 105, *130*

Number-family relationships: highlighting strips reinforcing, 102; triangular flash cards reinforcing, 95

Number line on a zipper, 86

Number Relationships, as math strategy, 92

Numbers in the News, as math strategy, 101

Numerical patterns: grids for visualizing, 105; Hundreds Chart for finding, 38, *130*

O

One, Two, Three…Go!, as assessment strategy, 110

One and Only Me, The, for advertising for one's own replacement, 33

"One Piece of the Puzzle" Grouping Method, for assigning group projects, 12

One Strip at a Time, as math strategy, 87

Online games and activities, for community building, 19

Origins Online website, 19

Overlays, for Scotopic Sensitivity Syndrome, 59, *133*

Over the Head, as literacy strategy, 77

P

Page protectors, for work sheets, 50

Parallel reading, teaching tools for, 41

Parent involvement, resources on, 150

Parents: homework tips for, 7, *124*; resources for, 150; at student-led conferences, 113

Partner Pair, as literacy strategy, 78

Pass It On, as literacy strategy, 79

PBS Kids website, 39

PBS LearningMedia website, 52

Pencil grips, for handwriting problems, 51

Personal-Learning Time Lines, as assessment strategy, 111

Phone book pages, for math practice, 100

Phoneme discrimination, difficulty with, 36

Phonics phone, as teaching tool, 36

Photo books, digital, for presentations, 18

Photo Peach website, 91

Photos, for learning math concepts, 91

Pick Your Presentation Style, for research projects, 18

Pic Lits website, 8

Pics4Learning website, 91

Place mats, for practicing math facts, 88

Plastic insects, as focusing tool, 45

Playing cards, for math games, 90

Plotting Homework, for establishing homework guidelines, 7, *124*

Podcasting using cell phones, 18

Point the Finger, for nonverbal signaling, 48

Poll the Audience, as assessment strategy, 108

Popsicle sticks, for calling on students, 14

Positive numbers, zipper for learning, 86

Positive talk: about other students, 24, 31; about self, 9

Poster placement, for activating visualization, 10

Posters, for presenting research projects, 18

"Post It" with Notes, 44

Post What You Know, as assessment strategy, 119

PowerPoint games and templates, online, 39

PowerPoint presentations, for research projects, 18

PowerPoint slides, clickers for responding to, 108

Power Up Your Center Time, interactive whiteboards for, 35

Note: Page numbers in italics indicate reproducibles to be used with strategies.

Praise, written on paper airplanes, 31

Praise Behind Your Back, for encouraging positive talk about students, 24

Presentation style, choosing, for research projects, 18

Presentation tools for students, online, 18

Pre-teaching, as literacy strategy, 58

Prezi website, 18

Print enlargement, as literacy strategy, 56

Problem reporting, 1, *122*

Procedural self-talk, 9

Processing content, writing activity for, 17

Professor Garfield website, 61

Promethean Planet website, 35

Puzzles: for assigning group projects, 12; websites for making, 8

Q

Questions, color-coding, as literacy strategy, 76

Quiet, Please! Student at Work, for blocking distractions, 55

Quizlet website, 8

Quiz Snack website, 117

R

R.A.F.T., digital, as literacy strategy, 65

Reading: aloud, improving comprehension from, 62; cards for responding to, 85; deepening understanding after, 61; differentiating instruction on, viii; difficulty crossing brain's midline when, 63; drawing scenes after, 81; enlarging print for, 56; finding main idea when, 83; independent, choosing books for, 79; journaling about, 74, *136*; news articles, 73; partners increasing fluency in, 78; resources on, 150–52; with Scotopic Sensitivity Syndrome, 59, *133*; sliding mask as focusing tool for, 47; Splash and Sort activity before, 72; sticky notes for responding to, 44, 80; summarizing passages from, 84; word clouds for, 67

Ready, Set, Create!, as literacy strategy, 61

Realistic Rubrics, as assessment strategy, 116

Records, Anecdotal, for tracking success of interventions, 107, *144*

Report card, alternative kind of, 114, *145*

Reporting problems, 1, *122*

Reports: differentiating writing assignments for, viii; puzzle grouping for, 12

Reproducibles, *122–45*; finding strategies matching, x, 121; locating, ix

Research projects, choosing presentation style for, 18

Resident Experts, using business cards to identify, 25

Resiliency, self-talk for building, 9

Resources, recommended, 146–54

Respect, toothpaste demonstration encouraging, 28

Response cards: for after-reading activity, 85; for assessing understanding of individual students, 106

Response tools: hand-held wireless, 108; highlighting tape, 43; response cards, 85, 106; sticky notes, 44, 80, 119

Rhymes: for learning in bite-size chunks, 64; as mnemonic device, 54

Right-handed students, eye directionality in, 10

Rubistar website, 18

Rubrics: for assessment, 116; for student presentations, 18

S

Sand timers, for teaching time orientation, 53

San Francisco Symphony Kids website, 8

Scaffolding, viii, 82

Scavenger Hunt(s): Digital, as literacy strategy, 82; Multiple Intelligence, for community building, 29, *128*

Science Kids website, 52

Science resources, 152

Scotopic Sensitivity Syndrome: overlays for, 59; self-test for, *133*

Scrabble, Human, as literacy strategy, 60

Seating locations, classroom, 2

Self-talk, positive and procedural, 9

Self-Test, for identifying Scotopic Sensitivity Syndrome, *133*

Shy students, seating choices of, 2

Simple K12 website, 69

Sitting in front of room, advantages of, 2

Skill Levels Students Can Deal With, as math strategy, 90

Slide show production, as literacy strategy, 57

Note: Page numbers in italics indicate reproducibles to be used with strategies.

Sliding Mask, as focusing tool, 47, *132*
Slower learners, classroom seating for, 2
SMART Exchange website, 35
SMART Response Systems website, 108
Smilebox website, 57, 91
Social studies resources, 152
Sound discrimination, helping students with difficulty in, 41
Special education resources, 152–53
Spelling website, 8
Spelling help, for English language learners, 75
Spelling practice, ensuring correct, 110
Spelling resources, 150–52
Splash and Sort, as literacy strategy, 72
Stand, Move, Deliver, for processing what's been learned, 17
Stethoscope, for parallel reading, 41
Sticky notes: online, for assessment, 119; as reading response tool, 44, 80
Sticky-Note Symbols, as literacy strategy, 80
Stocks, following, as math anchor activity, 101
Story writing, 4-6-8 strategy for, 68, *134*
Struggling students. *See also* Discouraged students: help for, 11, 55, 58, 109, *125*
Student at Work: Do Not Disturb, for avoiding visual distractions, 3
Student-Led Conferences, as assessment strategy, 113
Student names, on Popsicle sticks, 14
Student Problem Report, 122
Student to Student, as instruction-giving game, 16
Study Stack website, 8
Stuffed animal, telling problems to, 1
Subtraction problems: grid for, *140*; separating, from addition problems, 97
Success, "I Can" slips for recording, 15, *126*
Summaries, writing, 84
Survey Monkey website, 117
Survey Says, as assessment strategy, 117
Symbols, Sticky Note, as literacy strategy, 80

T

Tactile learners, Wikki Stix for, 37
Tagxedo website, 67
Talking tube, as teaching tool, 40
Talk to Yourself, for using phonics phone, 36
Task completion, self-talk for improving, 9

Tattling, minimizing, 1
Teacher's Guide, The, website, 69
Teach in Chunks, as literacy strategy, 64
Teaching tools: bingo chips as math counters, 38; ear protection for distracted students, 55; educational videos, 52; finger pointer, 48; focus frames, 46, *131*; for handwriting problems, 51; highlighting tape, 43; interactive whiteboard, 35; mnemonics, 54; mobile devices, 42; online games and templates, 39; page protectors, 50; phonics phone, 36; plastic insects, 45; Post-It Notes, 44; sand timers for time orientation, 53; sliding mask, 47, *132*; stethoscope or airplane headphone, 41; talking tube, 40; Wikki Stix for tactile or kinesthetic learners, 37; word catcher, 49
Teach with Edibles, as math strategy, 89, *137–38*
Team Windowpane Discussion, as literacy strategy, 81
Technology-based strategies: Choice Charts for selecting anchor activities, 8; for differentiated instruction, vii; digital comic strips as after-reading activity, 61; digital images for learning math concepts, 91; digital scavenger hunts for research, 82; educational videos, 52; interactive whiteboard as learning center, 35; movie or slide show production, 57; online bulletin boards for posting student responses, 119; online-created surveys, 117; online games and activities for community building, 19; online PowerPoint games and templates, 39; polling with hand-held wireless response devices, 108; presentation tools, 18, 65; reading online news articles, 73; video recordings, 112; virtual field trips, 69; wireless devices for, 42
10 Homework Tips for Parents, 7, *124*
There's an App for That, mobile devices and, 42
Three-Card Write, as literacy strategy, 85
Three Facts and a Fib, as literacy strategy, 71
Tiered activities, viii
Time, telling, 86, 94
Time Lines, Personal-Learning, as assessment strategy, 111
Time orientation problems, 53
Toasted Cheese website, 8
Tomlinson, Carol Ann, vii
Tongue depressors, for calling on students, 14

Note: Page numbers in italics indicate reproducibles to be used with strategies.

Toothpaste, for encouraging respectful communication, 28

Tracking, resources on, 153

Triangular flash cards, for reinforcing number-family relationships, 95

Triangular Number Bonds, 95

Tutorials, website on, 52

TweenTribune website, 73

Twist and Learn with Wikki Stix, 37

U

Ultimate Camp Resource website, 19

Untracking, resources on, 153

Using a Focus Frame to Get the Picture, for eliminating distractions, 46

Utah Education Network website, 69

V

Video recordings, as assessment strategy, 112

Videos, educational, 52

Virtual field trips, as literacy strategy, 69

Visual learners, help for, 91

Visual processing of information, eye directionality indicating, 10

Vocabulary building: active involvement for, 75; for English language learners, 40; headbands for, 77; resources on, 150–52; with Splash and Sort prereading activity, 72; word clouds for, 67; word map for, 70, *135*

Vocabulary Spelling City website, 8

Vocal Immersion, with stethoscope or airplane headphone, 41

Voice Thread website, 65

Voki website, 65

W

Walkway, Class, for encouraging students facing difficulties, 20

Wall Wisher website, 119

Watch and Learn, educational videos in, 52

WatchKnowLearn website, 52

Watch Your Tongue, for avoiding negative messages, 21

Websites, recommended, 153. *See also specific websites*

Well, I Never!, for identifying common interests, 34

We're Going on a Scavenger Hunt!, for identifying multiple intelligences, 29, *128*

What's My Name?, as math strategy, 96

What's Your Response?, as assessment strategy, 106

Whiteboard, interactive. *See* Interactive whiteboard

Wikki Stix, as teaching tool for tactile or kinesthetic learners, 37

Windowpaning, as literacy strategy, 81

Word catcher, for focusing attention, 49

Word Clouds, as literacy strategy, 67

Wordle website, 67

Word Map, as literacy strategy, 70, *135*

Word problems on math papers, eliminating, for non-readers and English language learners, 109

Work sheets, page protectors for, 50

World at Their Fingertips, The, as literacy strategy, 69

Writing. *See also* Handwriting: advertisement for one's own replacement, 33; difficulty crossing brain's midline when, 63; editing, 66; interactive, using highlighting tape with, 43; in journal (*see* Journaling); from perspective other than own, 65; Post-It Notes for revising or editing, 44; for processing content, 17; resources on, 150–52; responses to reading, 85; story, 4-6-8 strategy for, 68; summaries, 84; websites on, 8

Y

Yellow markers, for highlighting answers, 5

Yodio website, 18

You Can Count on Bingo Chips, for math activities, 38

Z

Zipper, for math calculations, 86

Zoomerang website, 117

Note: Page numbers in italics indicate reproducibles to be used with strategies.

Common Core State Standards Addressed by *Differentiated Instruction*

English Language Arts

Grades K–8

Reading

- Integrate and evaluate content presented in diverse media and formats, including visually and quantitatively, as well as in words.
- Determine central ideas or themes in a text.
- Read and analyze complex literary and informational texts.

Writing

- Develop and strengthen writing as needed by planning, revising, editing, rewriting, or trying a new approach.
- Use technology, including the Internet, to produce and publish writing and to interact and collaborate with others.
- Draw evidence from literary or informational texts to support analysis, reflection, and research.

Speaking and Listening

- Prepare for and participate effectively in a range of conversations and collaborations with diverse partners, building on others' ideas and expressing their own clearly and persuasively.
- Make strategic use of digital media and visual displays of data to express information and enhance understanding of presentations.

Language

- Demonstrate command of the conventions of standard English capitalization, punctuation, and spelling when writing.
- Apply knowledge of language to understand how language functions in different contexts, to make effective choices for meaning or style, and to comprehend more fully when reading or listening.
- Demonstrate understanding of figurative language, word relationships, and nuances in word meanings.

Common Core State Standards Addressed by
Differentiated Instruction

Mathematics

Grades K–2

- Use numbers to count, compare, add, subtract, measure, classify.
- Understand and apply properties of operations.
- Understand place value.
- Represent and interpret data.
- Identify, describe, analyze, compare, create, and compose shapes.

Grades 3–5

- Represent and solve problems with multiplication and division.
- Gain familiarity with factors and multiples.
- Write and interpret numerical expressions.
- Identify, generate, and analyze patterns.
- Use place value to perform multi-digit arithmetic.
- Develop understanding of fractions and decimals.
- Solve problems involving measurement.
- Tell and write time.
- Represent and interpret data.
- Identify and classify shapes based on their attributes and properties.

Grades 6–8

- Apply and extend previous understandings of addition, subtraction, multiplication, and division.
- Compute fluently with multi-digit numbers.
- Solve real-world mathematical problems.
- Use random sampling to draw inferences.

Other Differentiated Instruction Titles Available from Crystal Springs Books

Different Tools for Different Learners

Differentiated Math

Differentiating Instruction in a Whole-Group Setting (Grades 3–8)

Differentiating Instruction in a Whole-Group Setting (Grades 7–12)

Differentiating Textbooks

Engage All Students

The More Ways You Teach, The More Students You Reach